# BEHOLD THE SAVIOUR

## WARREN HENDERSON

GOSPEL FOLIO PRESS
www.gospelfolio.com

Published by GOSPEL FOLIO PRESS
304 Killaly St. West
Port Colborne, ON, L3K 6A6, Canada

ISBN 1-897117-27-2

Cover design by Rachel Brooks

All Scripture quotations from the King James
Version of the Bible unless otherwise noted.

Ordering Information:
GOSPEL FOLIO PRESS
Phone 1-800-952-2382
E-mail: order@gospelfolio.com
Web: www.gospelfolio.com

Printed in the United States of America

# Table of Contents

# Acknowledgements

The author is indebted to all those who contributed to the publishing of *Behold the Saviour*. I praise the Lord and thank Him for each of the following individuals and for their contributions: Randy Amos and David Dunlap for technical editing. Jane Biberstein for general editing. Annette Hanson and David Lindstrom for proofreading assistance.

# Foreword

The four Gospels present the Lord Jesus Christ to mankind in the only dignified manner that God has endorsed. In tracing those brief years of His earthly sojourn, each Gospel writer upholds a specific viewpoint of the Saviour, thus, exposing various distinct glories for our appreciation, reverence and remembrance. It is to be understood that the books of Matthew, Mark, Luke and John are not a harmonizing attempt to portray the life of Christ but four inexhaustible and unique themes of His person and attributes.

Christ's ministry was a manifestation of His person. To capture in a few words all the aspects of Christ's person, character, emotions and doings is exceedingly difficult – which is why the Gospels, as literature, gleam with divine inspiration – each is God's deposition of His Son. John mentions the limitations of pen and paper to declare the fullness of His person and work: *"And there are also many other things which Jesus did, the which, if they should be written every one, I suppose that even the world itself could not contain the books that should be written" (John 21:25).* The author acknowledges that the work in the reader's hand is simply a minute rendering of the overall glory of Christ – a droplet in a great expanse. There is no attempt in this book to provide an expositional analysis of the four Gospels, rather the goal is to convey an overview of the unique Gospel vantage points of Christ. Much distinction and discretion may be found within the Gospel accounts – this is for our greater appreciation of God's mind and admiration for His Son. *"O the depth of the riches both of the wisdom and knowledge of God!" (Rom. 11:33).*

We live in fast-paced days, and unfortunately, many Christians are satisfying their spiritual appetites with mere devotional tidbits and "how to" books. Outwardly, the Church of the 21st century is busy doing, but inwardly, our love of Christ wanes cold and lifeless. As the Church's affection for Christ fades, the branches in the Vine clamor and rattle with spiritual mediocrity. The only true motive for Christian service is pure sacrificial love for the Saviour. If we do not love Christ, we cannot abide in Him – we cannot do anything to please Him. *"I am the vine, ye are the branches: He that abideth in Me, and I in him, the same bringeth forth much fruit: for without Me ye can do nothing" (John 15:5).*

Charles Haddon Spurgeon once said, "The more you know about Christ, the less you will be satisfied with superficial views of Him." The more we know of Christ, the more we will love Him, and the more we will experience Him. This study has refreshed my soul. In the long hours of contemplating the vast worth that the Father attaches to every aspect of the Saviour's life, I have been encouraged to love Him more. If you're feeling a bit dry or spiritually despondent, *"Behold the Saviour"* afresh – the Holy Spirit will ignite your passion for the Christ and invigorate your ministry for Him.

Not I, but Christ, be honored, loved, exalted;
Not I, but Christ, be seen, be known, be heard;
Not I, but Christ, in every look and action;
Not I, but Christ, in every thought and word.
Oh to be saved from myself, dear Lord, Oh to be lost in Thee,
Oh, that it may be no more I, But Christ that lives in me.

Mrs. A. A. Whiddington

# The Gospel Accounts

The phrase "I love you" is often uttered or penned to express fond tenderness and deep appreciation for another person. What speech or literary device, however, would one use to convey paramount enthusiasm and affection for another? "I really really love you" is a bit longer but is still only a mere attempt to arouse profound emotions through a singular and inadequate means. Perhaps, you wanted to demonstrate genuine devotion for another through the giving of a priceless gift; what affirmation would accompany your present? What substance of thought or fusion of words would effectively conspire to declare your heart's aspiration? How do you express boundless and fathomless love? God chose to confirm His vast love for us through the giving of His only begotten Son. God expressed His immutable and abundant love for humanity by His Son and in His Son. His only Son became His personal messenger and message of love to mankind.

> *God, who at sundry times and in divers manners spake in time past unto the fathers by the prophets, **hath in these last days spoken unto us by His Son**, whom He hath appointed heir of all things, by whom also He made the worlds; Who being the brightness of His glory, and the express image of His person, and upholding all things by the word of His power, when He had by Himself purged our sins, sat down on the right hand of the Majesty on high (Heb. 1:1-3).*

God demonstrated love to us through His Son: *"But God commendeth His love toward us, in that, while we were yet sinners, Christ died for us" (Rom. 5:8).* "For God so loved the world, that He gave His only begotten Son, that whosoever believeth in Him should not perish, but have everlasting life" *(John 3:16).* On the day of the Lord's transfiguration, the heavens opened, and the Father audibly declared, *"This is my beloved Son, in whom I am well pleased, hear ye Him" (Matt. 17:5).* Our Creator is a communicating God. He demonstrated and declared His ultimate love for us through the Living Word, the Lord Jesus Christ.

## A New Literary Form

God understands our natural limitations to comprehend spiritual and eternal matters. As a declaration of grace to us, He exercised various literary forms in the Old Testament, including word-pictures, prophecies, shadows, types, allegories, symbols, and plain language, to prelude the revelation of His supreme gift of love – His own Son to the world. This would allow humanity to both recognize Christ and freely accept His offer of salvation when He arrived. Then, in the New Testament, God demonstrated His infinite wisdom by creating a new and vivid literary form to express the grandeur of His Son's life and sacrifice. The new literary form is the "Gospel." So great would be this love revelation to the world that only the "Gospel" could declare the "mystery of godliness" – God manifest in the flesh. The four Gospels present the Lord Jesus Christ in the manner by which His Father chose to reveal Him. Let us *Behold the Saviour* in the way the Father deemed essential!

Concerning the literary content of the "Gospel," William MacDonald writes:

Everyone who has studied literature is familiar with the story, the novel, the play, the poem, and the biography, as well as other literary forms. But when our Lord Jesus Christ came to earth, a whole new category of literature was needed – the Gospel. The Gospels are not biographies, though they have strong biographical material. They are not stories, though they contain parables such as the Prodigal Son and the Good Samaritan that are as interesting as any story in all literature.… The Gospels are not documentary reports, yet they contain accurate, though obviously condensed, accounts of many conversations and discourses of our Lord.[1]

## The Meaning of Gospel

The word "Gospel" is found 101 times in the New Testament. In the original language, the noun form *euaggelion* simply means "a good message," while the verb form *euaggelizo* refers to "announcing the good news," or "to evangelize." The Gospel message is good news from heaven to all humanity. The good news is that, through Christ, God's peace would come to mankind, or as the angelic host declared to the bewildered shepherds near Bethlehem so long ago, *"Glory to God in the highest, and on earth peace, good will, toward men" (Luke 2:14).* Samuel Ridout comments to the significance of this message and the unique fashion in which God conveyed it to humanity:

It is the consideration of such amazing and wondrous themes as these which make the four Gospels unique in the entire Word of God. These give us the history of the incarnation, and show us **"that Eternal Life which was with the Father and was manifested unto us."** The Epistles give us the precious truths which flow from the great fact of the incarnation and the Cross, but the Gospels show us the Person Himself, how He lived and how He died. There must therefore be a special importance attaching to this narrative. No other part of the New Testament could be substituted for the Gospels.[2]

## Uniqueness of the Gospels

As one examines the four Gospels (Matthew, Mark, Luke and John), it is quickly observed that deliberate variations, exclusions and inclusions of content exist within each account. There are different styles of language and arrangement of subjects. The Spirit of God obviously never intended for there to be a multiplication of narratives, but rather a necessity for variation. Likewise, the Holy Spirit made no attempt to convey a complete biography of the Lord's life, for lengthy gaps of personal history are apparent.

A brief breakdown of the content matter within the four Gospels will clearly demonstrate this point. Of the eighty-nine chapters in the four accounts, eighty-five pertain to the Lord's last three years on earth, and twenty-eight of these focus solely on His final week of ministry, His crucifixion, and His resurrection. Therefore, roughly one third of the four Gospels is devoted to the specific details surrounding the events of Calvary. The Gospel focus is a Person, not a biography of a person. The Gospels contain both the wisdom of God in sacred expression and what the Father longs for us to appreciate – the profound excellencies of His Son. C. I. Scofield summarizes the main purpose of the four Gospels:

The four Gospels record the eternal being, human ancestry, birth, life and ministry, death, resurrection, and ascension of Jesus the Christ, Son of God and Son of Man. Taken together, they set forth, not a biography but a Person.

The fact that the four Gospels present a Person rather than a complete biography indicates the spirit in which they should be approached. What is most important is to see and know through these narratives Him whom they reveal. It is of less importance to endeavor to piece together a full account of His life from these inspired records (John 21:25). For some adequate reason it did not please God to cause to be written a full biography of His Son. The years up to the beginning of His ministry are passed over in a silence that is broken but once, and that in a few verses in Luke's Gospel (Luke 2:40-52). It is wise to respect the divine silence.

But the four Gospels, though designedly incomplete as a story, are complete as a revelation. We may not know everything that Jesus did, but we may know Him. In four great narratives, each of which in some respects supplements the other three, we have Jesus Christ Himself.[3]

## Harmony of the Gospels?

God's written "good news" to mankind is presented from the four unique vantage points of Christ found in Matthew, Mark, Luke and John. Many have tried in vain to fully harmonize these Gospel accounts, but they cannot be fully harmonized; each Gospel stands alone as an inspired testimony of a unique theme of Christ's life and ministry. On this subject, Samuel Ridout remarks as follows:

Had God intended that we should have but one narrative, He would have given us the record of the life of our Lord in that form. Our attention, therefore, should be directed to each separate Gospel to ascertain, as far as we may, its general character; its main theme; its point of view; the manner in which it presents our Lord.[4]

A. T. Robertson wrote a classic reference work entitled *A Harmony of the Gospels*. He acknowledges the difficulty of harmonizing the Gospels in the preface of that book:

> A harmony of the Gospels cannot meet every phase of modern criticism…. No effort is made to reconcile all the divergent statements of various details in the different Gospels. The differences challenge the student's interest as much as the correspondences and are natural marks of individual work.[5]

The intended purpose and distinct content of each of the four Gospels must be understood to more fully appreciate what God has *spoken unto us by* [His] *Son (Heb. 1:2)*. J. G. Bellett notes:

> The four Gospels are coincident testimonies to the Lord Jesus Christ, and valuable as such. But we are not to read them as merely explanatory or supplemental. We get a complete view of our Lord Jesus Christ only by discerning their distinctness in character and purpose.

> Even in the histories of men we may perceive this. One biographer may give us the man in his domestic, another in his political life; but in order to be fully acquainted with him, we must see him in both of these, and perhaps in many other connections. And one of such biographers will not only select particular facts, but notice distinct circumstances in the same facts. The same thing we see in the four Gospels.[6]

## Division of the Gospels

The symbolic scriptural meaning of number four will be more fully developed in the next chapter; it suffices here to introduce it as a number of **earthly order**. The number **four** is the first number that is divisible (4 ÷ 2 = 2). But in Scripture God rarely **divides** four in this way to reveal divine mysteries; He normally combines the numbers **one** and **three** to create four. F. W. Grant explains the scriptural observation:

> But these four Gospels are...not 2 and 2, which would be true division, and the Son of God cannot be in fact divided. But they are a 3 and 1, the divine numbers being brought out thus: how truly the effect of these part-representations to bring out the divine glory of the Man, Christ Jesus, every believing heart bears witness. The Synoptic Gospels, as they are called, stand thus as the first part here: Matthew with its testimony to the King, Mark to the Ministering Servant, Luke to the Man; clearly united among themselves, and proportionately distinct from John's testimony to the Word made flesh. Yet these three, as their number intimates, also declare, each after its own manner, God in Christ. It surely must be so, or there would be discord, not united witness.[7]

By devising a **three and one** Gospel format, God has upheld the symbolic scriptural meanings of the number **one** and **three** to represent His Son to the world. Number **one** represents divine unity and speaks of the Creator, while the number **three** signifies divine fullness and perfection. God used two **holy numbers** (numbers pertaining to Himself) to manifest the divine glory of His Son in the Gospels.

## Construction of the Gospels

Generally speaking, Matthew and Luke do not strive to record events in sequence, but in accordance with their associated themes of royalty and humanity, respectively. For this cause miracles, discourses, events, and related facts are grouped together to ensure the fullest development of the deliberate theme of the Holy Spirit. Mark provides the most concise and most chronologically accurate Gospel account; He is upholding the "doings" of the Lord. John would be the next most chronological account of the Lord's ministry but is characterized by vast gaps in the life of Christ. As William Kelly explains, it is the differences within the Gospels that call our attention to particular topical truths:

> If we suppose two facts, mutually illustrating each other, but occurring at totally different times, in such a case these two facts might be brought together. For instance, supposing the Spirit of God desired in our Lord's history to show the value of the word of God and of prayer, He might clearly bring together two remarkable occasions, in one of which our Lord revealed the mind of God about prayer – in the other, his judgment of the value of the word. The question whether the two events took place at the same time is here entirely immaterial. No matter when they occurred, they are here seen together; put out of the order of their occurrence, in fact, it is to form the justest order for illustrating the truth that the Holy Ghost meant us to receive.[8]

Matthew and John were personally discipled by Christ, while Mark and Luke were not. God employed quite a variety of writers and styles to portray His Son to the World. Two were Apostles; one was a Gentile believer, and one a later Jewish convert to Christ. One of the Apostles and one of the non-apostles recorded the events, generally, as they happened, while the remaining two upheld the richness of unique presentation. Andrew Jukes offers an explanation for this means of exaltation and expression:

> The fact is that our perceptions do not grasp realities, but their form. If therefore what is seen is to be described, we must have many representations even of the same object; and

this not only because the same object may be viewed on different sides, but because the amount of what is seen even on the same side will depend on the light and capacity of the beholder. He who made us knew this and provided for it. Hence of old, in type and figure, we have view after view of Him who was to come; not only because His offices and perfections were many, but also because we were weak and needed such a revelation.

Thus in the single relationship of offering, Christ is seen a Burnt-offering, Peace-offering, and Sin-offering [also a Meal-offering and Trespass-offering], each but a different view of the same one offering; each of which again may be seen in various measures, and yet the offering itself is only one. And just as the self-same act of dying on the cross, our Lord was at the same moment a sweet-savor offering, willingly offering to God a perfect obedience, and also a sin-offering, penal bearing the judgement due to sin, and as such made a curse for us; so in the selfsame acts of His life, each act may be seen in different aspects, for each act has a Divine fullness. It is this fullness which God in mercy presents to our view in the diversities of the Four Gospels.

It is for this reason that a Harmony of the Gospels, though it is interesting and has its uses, leads us from the special purpose for which the Gospels were written as they are.[9]

The unique Gospel themes preclude a full harmony of facts but serve as an invitation to appreciate the distinct glories of Christ's holy character, divine essence, and selfless ministry. As one slowly rotates a prism immersed in white light, various colors are refracted through the prism, such that the color one actually sees will depend upon the viewpoint from which one gazes upon the prism. Same prism, same light, but distinctions in radiance are observed from various on-looking positions. As we view the Lord Jesus Christ by the light of divine revelation, we learn to appreciate the fullness of His matchless splendor from the diverse Gospel illuminations. The Son is thoroughly and altogether lovely, as the Father fittingly proclaims to us through the four Gospel records.

> And as to the ways of the blessed Lord which are, in this variety, given to us, I need not say that all is perfection. Whether it be this path or that which He takes before us – whatever relationship He sustains – whatever affection fills His soul – though different, all is perfect. He may pass before us in the conscious elevation of the Son of God, or in the sympathies of the Son of man; we may see Him in Jewish connection, in St. Matthew; or more widely abroad, as among men, in St. Luke; as the Servant of the varied need of sinners, in St. Mark; or as the solitary Stranger from heaven, in St. John; still, all is perfection. And to discern and trace this, is at once the disciple's profit and delight. "Thy testimonies are wonderful; therefore doth my soul keep them."[10]

– J. G. Bellett

# Why Four Gospels?

Perhaps, to some, this question may seem strange, as the four Gospels have been read, studied, and cherished for nearly two millennia. Unfortunately, many have missed **why** we have four and **what** each was to specifically teach through their own intrinsic peculiarities. There is as much divine wisdom presented in what is proclaimed in the Gospels as in what is not. The Spirit of God inspired the variations, as much as He did the conforming characteristics of the Gospel accounts. What a solicitation to explore divine reason and distinctive design! What an opportunity to wonder at supreme intellect! What an omnipotent and all wise God!

So, why not two Gospels? Why not five Gospel accounts? Why four? Because two accounts, or three, or five, or anything else but four, would not provide a perfect presentation of the varying glories of the blessed Saviour. The giving of Christ as the substitutional sin bearer for mankind was not an afterthought of God; it was planned before anything was created (1 Pet. 1:18-20). The foreordained counsel of God determined the divine presentation of Christ in Scripture. The whole of the Old Testament thus prepares the way of Christ's coming to earth through the proclamation of hundreds of prophecies, shadows and types.

## Concerning Typology

By the word **type**, we simply mean a picture, figure, or pattern that reflects something or someone in reality. The word "type" or "print" comes from the Greek word *tupos*. It is used to speak of the nail "print" in the Lord's hand (John 20:25) and of the tabernacle furniture which was to be fashioned according to the "pattern" given Moses in the mount (Heb. 8:5). Thomas said he would not believe that the Lord had been raised up unless he felt the print of the nail in the Lord's hand. In other words, the pattern left in the Lord's hand would match the nail, yet it was not the nail. However, the print furnished evidence of what the nail was like (size and shape). Likewise, Scripture is saturated with "types" of Christ. These offer evidence of Christ, but are not Christ. There is no perfect "type" or "pattern," or it would be the real thing. Therefore, all types, foreshadows, symbols, analogies, and patterns are inadequate to express fully and completely every aspect of His person and work.

Biblical **typology** and **numerology** have perhaps suffered more at the hands of overzealous theologians than by those who would undermine their proper use. Though a hermeneutical defense of these interpretation methods is beyond the scope of this book, some fundamental definitions are appropriate. **Numerology** focuses its attention upon the symbolic meaning of numbers beyond their normally understood numerical significance. In biblical study, numerology forms a portion of the broader study called **typology**. Concerning **typology,** John Walvoord affords a concise definition:

> A *type* may be defined as an exceptional Old Testament reality which was specially ordained by God effectively to prefigure a single New Testament redemptive truth.[1]

14

Typology is thus a form of prophetic statement. It differs from prophecy in that it may be discerned as typological only after its fulfillment is known. Once this antitype is revealed, one may look back and see that certain expressions and images have meanings besides the historical experience.[2]

F. W. Grant acknowledges the proper use of and, indeed, need for typology to understand the fullness of what God has revealed to mankind through Scripture:

Some would have us stop where the inspired explanation stops. But in that case, how large a part of what is plainly symbolical would be lost to us! – the larger part of the Levitical ordinances, not a few of the parables of the Lord himself, and almost the whole of the book of Revelation. Surely none could deliberately accept a principle which would lock up from us so large a part of the inspired Word.

Still many have the thought that it would be safer to refrain from typical applications of the historical portions where no inspired statement authenticates them as types at all. Take, however, such a history as that of Joseph, which no direct Scripture speaks of as a type, yet the common consent of almost all receives as such; or Isaac's sacrifice, of the significance of which we have the least hint. The more we consider it, the more we find it impossible to stop short here. Fancy, no doubt, is to be dreaded. Sobriety and reverent caution are abundantly needful. But so are they every where. If we profess wisdom, we become fools: subjection to the blessed Spirit of God, and to the Word inspired of Him, are our only safeguards here and elsewhere.

When we look a little closer, we find that the types are not scattered by hap-hazard in the Old Testament books. On the contrary, they are connected together and arranged in an order and with a symmetry which bear witness to the divine hand which has been at work throughout. We find Exodus thus to be the book of redemption; Leviticus, to speak of what suits God with us in the sanctuary of sanctification, then Numbers, to give the wilderness history – our walk with God (after redemption and being brought to Him where He is,) through the world. Each individual type in these different books will be found to have most intimate and significant relation to the great central thought pervading the book. This, when laid hold of, confirms immensely our apprehension of the general and particular meaning, and gives it a force little if at all short of absolute demonstration.[3]

Though most numbers in Scripture have a literal meaning (For example: Christ arose from the grave on the **third** day.), some numbers serve a purely figurative purpose. The Lamb with **seven** horns in Revelation 5:6 symbolically represents the Lord's omnipotence (**Seven** is the number of perfection, and a **horn** represents **power** in Scripture.). Sometimes both a figurative and a literal meaning may be understood, especially when the obvious literal sense is within a personal narrative and the figurative sense conveys a future meaning verified elsewhere in Scripture. For example, the seven-year famine in Joseph's day was both an actual devastating famine that literally affected the whole land and a forewarning of a yet future seven year tribulation period that would devastate the entire planet. It is noted that **Egypt** figuratively speaks of "the world" in Scripture.

Numbers **one** through **forty** and many numbers above forty are used in a repeated figurative manner in the Bible to show a particular meaning. This figurative repetition is one of many evidences which demonstrates that all Scripture comes from one Mind – it is God-breathed (2 Tim. 3:16). For example, in Genesis 2:1-3, we are first introduced to the number "seven." From the beginning, the number **seven** is God's number and a fundamental building block which speaks of "perfection" or "completeness." The word "sanctified," also appearing for the first time in these verses, means "set apart" or "holy." The week of creation ended on the seventh day with a day of rest for the Lord. This rest was a divine response to His satisfaction with His creative work, not to weariness (Isa. 40:28). God literally declared seven times in Genesis 1 that what He had created was **good**, but also declared through the use of the number seven that it was **perfect.**

## The Number "Four"

What about the number **four**? How is **four** generally used in a figurative sense in the Bible? The number "four" is the number of **earthly order**, as created by God. Here are a few expressions of the number four in Scripture, all of which have earthly significance. There are...

**Four** seasons (Spring, Summer, Fall and Winter).
**Four** regions/directions, (north, south, east, and west).
**Four** divisions of day (morning, noon, evening, and night).
**Four** phases of the moon (new, half waxing, full, half waning).
**Four** winds (from the four directions of the earth).
**Four** realms in which creatures dwell (upon the earth, under the earth, in the heaven, or in the sea).
**Four** means of dividing the human race (kindred, people, tongue, and nation).
**Four** types of soils to reflect the hearts of all men (hard, stony, thorny, and good unto fruitfulness).

F. W. Grant offers this insight into the symbolic meaning of the number "four" in Scripture:

The number 4 is the first one capable of true division, and which the number 2 divides. This gives it its character. It is significant of that which *yields itself up to this division, as material to the hand that fashions it.* It is thus the number of the world, and implies *weakness* necessarily, therefore, which may give way under trial, and yield to another hand than the One who has title over it. And this the creature has done. Therefore the world is what it is today, and all the trial and evil of which it is the scene.[4]

How does **four** then relate to God's presentation of His Son to humanity? When the Son exited the dimensionless and timeless realm of majesty on high and descended to the earth, He willingly placed Himself under earthly order. As a man, He became subject to the natural laws of creation, even though, as God, He still maintained the order of all things (Col. 1:17). Consequently, the Lord never allowed His deity to satisfy His humanity beyond the normal scope in which all humanity experiences the daily blessings of God. Many other means are employed in Scripture to convey relevance to the Lord's condescending journey to earth for the sole purpose of suffering death, that mankind might have an opportunity to be restored to a holy God. For example, the Lord Jesus referred to Himself more often by the title "Son of Man" than by the title "Son of God." In so doing, He was not calling attention to His divine essence but to His lowly position and ministry on earth. The Spirit of God, throughout the Bible, consistently represents the glories of the Son, while being **earthly-connected**, by employing the number **four**.

Before exploring the Old Testament for representations of Christ from the earthly number of four, it is plainly noted that each of the four Gospels upholds the brilliancy of the Lord both from a different perspective and to a unique earthly audience. The following table provides a short summary to assist in recognizing more clearly the Old Testament four-fold pictures of the coming Saviour to earth.

| Gospel | Matthew | Mark | Luke | John |
|---------|---------|---------|----------|-----------|
| Perspective | King | Servant | Humanity | Deity |
| Audience | Jewish | Roman | Greek | The World |

## The Four Rivers

Normally, water flows in a similar direction from one geographic location to a lower position, but this apparently was not the case for the river that went out of the Garden of Eden.

*Now a river went out of Eden to water the garden, and from there it parted and became four riverheads. The name of the first is Pishon; it is the one which skirts the whole land of Havilah, where there is gold. And the gold of that land is good. Bdellium and the onyx stone are there. The name of the second river is Gihon; it is the one which goes around the whole land of Cush. The name of the third river is Hiddekel; it is the one which goes toward the east of Assyria. The fourth river is the Euphrates (Gen. 2:10-14, NKJV).*

Prior to the fall of mankind, God dwelt in Eden with Adam and his wife (later named Eve). The number **one** symbolizes **unity**. Adam and Eve were **one flesh** and **one with God** in the sense that complete unity and peaceful fellowship characterized the garden scene prior to sin. Thus, in Eden, where God dwelt happily with man, only one river is observed. Similarly, only **one** street of gold will be found in heaven (Rev. 21:21) – there is only **one way** to enter into full fellowship with God (John 14:6). Noah's ark had only **one** door. Likewise, God commanded that there be only one entrance into either the temple or the tabernacle. However, after the river flowed out of

Eden, it became **four** rivers and watered the **whole land.** Other than the mention of the fourth day of creation, this is the first direct reference to the number "four" in the Bible. It is used, with the number **one**, to symbolize departure from God's dwelling place (paradise) to an earthly domain apart from His intimate fellowship.

If the references to geography, as stated in Genesis 2, remained somewhat the same after the flood, Eden would then have been in the Persian Gulf region and, more specifically, in modern-day Iraq. If this assertion is correct, what is of further interest is that the Pishon would have flowed northwesterly, the Gihon southwesterly, the Hiddekel northeasterly, and the Euphrates, as it does today, southeasterly. Literally the whole land, in every direction, received that blessing which flowed out from God's presence.

Speaking to Abraham, God said, *"I will bless them that bless thee, and curse him that curseth thee: and in thee shall **all families of the earth** be blessed" (Gen. 12:3).* The writer of Hebrews, speaking of the Lord, writes, *"But we see Jesus, who was made a little lower than the angels for the suffering of death, crowned with glory and honor; that He by the grace of God **should taste death for every man" (Heb 2:9).*** The Apostle John declares of Christ, *"And He is the propitiation for our sins: and not for ours only, but also for the sins of the whole world" (1 Jn. 2:2). "For God so loved **the world,** that He gave His only begotten Son!"* When the Son withdrew from the realms of glory to accomplish His humbling mission on earth, He brought a divine blessing of the richest kind to **the whole of humanity** – Himself.

## The Four "Beholds"

Four unique "behold" statements are found within the Old Testament that prepare the way for Christ's first earthly advent;

each one emphasizes one of the main Gospel themes. "Behold" means "to earnestly look upon with regard"; it may convey a connotation of surprise or wonder. These four "Behold" statements are God the Father's invitation to mankind to gaze upon and admire His dear Son.

*Rejoice greatly, O daughter of Zion! Shout, O daughter of Jerusalem!* **Behold, your King** *is coming to you; He is just and having salvation, lowly and riding on a donkey, A colt, the foal of a donkey (Zech. 9:9, NKVJ).*

**Behold My Servant,** *whom I uphold; Mine elect, in whom My soul delighteth; I have put My spirit upon Him: He shall bring forth judgment to the Gentiles (Isa. 42:1).*

*And speak unto him, saying, Thus speaketh the Lord of hosts, saying,* **Behold the Man** *whose name is The Branch; and He shall grow up out of His place, and He shall build the temple of the Lord (Zech 6:12).*

*O Zion, that bringest good tidings, get thee up into the high mountain; O Jerusalem, that bringest good tidings, lift up thy voice with strength; lift it up, be not afraid; say unto the cities of Judah,* **Behold your God!** *(Isa. 40:9).*

> Behold your King – Gospel of Matthew
> Behold My Servant – Gospel of Mark
> Behold the Man – Gospel of Luke
> Behold your God – Gospel of John

When the Lord is presented in a position of authority (as King and as God), the possessive pronoun "your" precedes the title, but when the position of a lowly servant is stated, the pronoun "My" appears. When the Lord is introduced in the intermediate stature, as a man, however, the neutral "the" is applied. This arrangement demonstrates the various facets and positional glories of the Lord's ministry and how He would relate to mankind. As a man, the Lord is on an equal footing with humanity, though, spiritually speaking, He was and is alive and all of mankind was then dead. In Matthew and John, the Lord is presented in a position of authority above man. In Mark, the Lord, in accordance to the will of the Father, humbly lowered Himself (not in essence, but in the sense of position) below the rightful station of divinity and took on the form of a Servant.

*Who, being in the form of God, thought it not robbery to be equal with God: But made Himself of no reputation, and took upon Him the form of a servant, and was made in the likeness of men: And being found in fashion as a man, He humbled Himself, and became obedient unto death, even the death of the cross (Phil. 2:6-8).*

Within the New Testament, two "behold" statements frame the beginning and ending moments of the Lord's ministry on earth. John the Baptist, who prepared the way for the Lord's coming, proclaimed in reference to the Lord Jesus, *"**Behold the Lamb of God**, which taketh away the sin of the world" (John 1:29).* Just hours before the death of our Lord, after He had been mocked, buffeted, scourged, and spit upon, Pilate presented Jesus to the Jews, *"**Behold, your King!**" (John 19:14).* It was a gruesome presentation. Thorns had breached the Lord's brow. His beard had been wrenched from His face as an undesired weed is uprooted and discarded from a garden. Roman fists had pulverized His comely visage in playful sport. What King is this? The prophet Isaiah, writing seven centuries earlier, foretold the sufferings of the Saviour at this moment. He would be so physically marred by human brutality, that He would cease to resemble human form (Isa. 52:14). Any movie's portrayal of these events or any artist's conception of this scene will be incredibly sanitized from the gory reality. Isaiah also declared what the Jewish attitude towards their God-sent Messiah would be upon that hallowed day, *"When we shall see Him, there is no beauty that we should desire Him" (Isa. 53:2).* So, when presented with their king, the Jews emphatically shouted, *"We have no king, but Caesar" (John 19:15).*

## The Four Branches

The sacrifice of unblemished animals is most often used to typify the sinless life of the Lord Jesus being poured out at Calvary in the Old Testament. God initiated this representation when He killed innocent animals in order to provide skins to cover the nakedness of Adam and Eve after the fall. Abel offered the firstling of his flock as a sweet-smelling sacrifice to God and understood that it pleased God, so he continued the practice by faith, trusting in God that it would be well with him.

However, in some cases, non-living objects such as a water-issuing rock, a fixed nail, a bronze serpent on a pole, or the tabernacle furnishings portray other aspects of the Lord's character or work. Occasionally, non-conscious living things are used to symbolize some aspect of the Lord's activities. Examples would include a fruit-bearing vine, an olive tree, or the gopher trees used by Noah and his family to build an ark to escape the imminent flood.

Before the ark could be constructed, building materials were needed – trees had to be cut down. The death of these trees pictured the humanity of Christ in that only through His sacrifice could spiritual life for man be secured. But since trees don't have blood, God is careful to apply some to the ark that we not miss the fuller picture. The word translated as "pitch" in Genesis 6:14 is most often translated "atonement" (nearly 75 times in the Old Testament). Prior to Calvary, man's sin could only be atoned (covered) by the blood of animals through sacrifices. The fact that the ark was pitched from within and without further shadows the future suffering and sacrifice of Christ. From His wounds, redemptive blood would rudely and profusely coat his outer skin then drip and splatter upon the ground. The word usage and the typology of Genesis 6 both convey the visage of a bleeding ark, thus, picturing the suffering Man of Calvary.

The humanity of Christ is again symbolized by wood in the tabernacle furnishings. God commanded, as recorded in Exodus 25-27, that the Ark of the Covenant, the Golden Altar of Incense, the Table of Showbread, and the boards that formed the walls of the tabernacle all be made of wood overlaid with gold. In the figurative sense, gold in Scripture speaks of purity and holiness. In the Tabernacle, the gold and the wood combine to express the full deity and full humanity of Christ.

Aaron's budding and fruitful rod of Numbers 17, while in the midst of all the other dead rods, declares the Lord Jesus as *"the resurrection and the life" (John 11:25).* Paul proclaimed that Christ was the first fruits from the dead; He is the first man to have experienced glorification, but a harvest of faithful souls is yet to follow (1 Cor. 15:20).

In the Old Testament, the Lord speaks prophetically of His Son being a Branch in four ways, which align with the unique vantage points of Christ in the four Gospels:

> *Behold, the days come, saith the Lord, that **I will raise unto David a righteous Branch, and a King** shall reign and prosper, and shall execute judgment and justice in the earth (Jer. 23:5,* also see Isa. 11:1).

*Hear now, O Joshua the high priest, thou, and thy fellows that sit before thee: for they are men wondered at: for, behold, **I will bring forth my Servant the Branch** (Zech. 3:8).*

*And speak unto him, saying, Thus speaketh the Lord of hosts, saying, **Behold the Man whose name is the Branch**; and He shall grow up out of His place, and He shall build the temple of the Lord (Zech. 6:12).*

***In that day shall the Branch of the Lord be beautiful and glorious**, and the fruit of the earth shall be excellent and comely for them that are escaped of Israel (Isa. 4:2).*

The four divine titles of the Lord perfectly align with the four Gospel presentations of Christ:

Unto David a Branch ... a King – Gospel of Matthew
My Servant, the Branch – Gospel of Mark
The Man ... the Branch – Gospel of Luke
The Branch of the Lord – Gospel of John

## The Four Faces

The apostle Paul confirms that God has shown Himself to all men through creation – creation demands a Creator. Consequently, man has no excuse for worshipping the creature instead of the Creator; to do so is not ignorance but resolute rebellion. *"For the invisible things of Him from the creation of the world are clearly seen, being understood by things that are made, even His eternal power and Godhead, so that they are without excuse" (Rom. 1:20).* In fact, all creation, visible or invisible, provides a wonderful testimony of God's greatness. *"Bless the Lord, all His works in all places of His dominion: bless the Lord, O my soul" (Ps. 103:22).* Included are spiritual beings in heavenly realms, which continually declare the glory of God and praise His name (Ps. 103:20).

The Bible informs us that classes of spiritual beings do indeed exist in heaven for this very purpose. Besides Michael the archangel, there are cherubim, seraphim, the four living creatures, and a host of innumerable angels with various functions and roles; for example, the angel Gabriel announced the births of both the Lord Jesus and John the Baptist. Furthermore, God describes to us what many of these spiritual beings do and how they appear before God's throne in heaven. All things recorded in Scripture have a divine purpose, so why did God go to the effort of affording these details? What is it that He wants us to learn?

It is my opinion that the Father is calling our attention to His Son through the appearance of these created beings. When the cherubim and seraphim cover themselves, it is for the purpose of concealing competing glories in God's presence – only God's glory will shine forth, for He alone is to be adored and worshipped in heaven. However, when the feet, eyes, or faces of these creatures are described, it is because they are not covered and, in fact, should not be, for some emulated glory of Christ is being proclaimed. This exercise of revealing and concealing glories is something that the Church is to remember and practice now on earth; in so doing, we pattern the holy scene in heaven (1 Cor. 11:2-16).

The scriptural accounts of the cherubim in Ezekiel 1 and 10, of the seraphim in Isaiah 6, and of the four living creatures in Revelation 4 all disclose that these beings have the same faces – four kinds of faces to be more exact. Apparently, the cherubim each have all four, that is, the face of a lion, the face of an ox, the face of a man, and the face of an eagle. The faces of these beings reflect the same glories of the Lord Jesus that are presented in the main themes of each Gospel. The **lion** is the king of the beasts, which reflects Matthew's perspective. The **ox**, as a beast of burden, is harnessed for the rigors of serving, and pictures Mark's presentation. The face of the **man** clearly agrees with Luke's prevalent theme of the Lord's humanity. Lastly, the **eagle** flies high above all the other creatures – in view is the divine essence of the Saviour.

The four faces of the cherubim, seraphim, and the four living creatures as seen in heaven:

> Lion – King – Gospel of Matthew
> Ox – Servant – Gospel of Mark
> Man – Humanity – Gospel of Luke
> Eagle – Deity – Gospel of John

## The Fours of the Tabernacle

Only one furnishing was to be within the **Most Holy Place** of the tabernacle, the Ark of the Covenant. God remained with the Israelites in the wilderness after He had delivered them from Egypt. He dwelt above the Mercy Seat that covered the Ark of the Covenant. There was but **one** Most Holy Place, **one** Ark and **one** Mercy Seat, but moving from the glorious presence of God to the realm occupied by men, a steady presentation of the number **four** is plainly observed.

Four different colored fabrics were woven together to make the tabernacle (the ceiling), which then had three more coverings placed upon it to make a total of four layers. The inner veil hung upon four pillars (Ex. 26:31-32) forming a barrier between the Most Holy Place where God dwelt and the holy place where the priests entered twice daily. The veil itself was woven with four different colored fabrics and displayed the figures of cherubim; cherubim each have four wings. Moving into the holy place we notice that the Golden Altar of Incense has four horns extended upward from the altar. Both the holy ointment, dabbed on parts of the tabernacle, and the prepared incense, placed twice daily by a priest upon the Golden Altar, were composed of four spices each.

Venturing eastward through the holy place into the courtyard, four more horns are noted upon the Bronze Altar. Peering eastward beyond the Bronze Altar, the only entrance to the tabernacle courtyard is seen, which is formed by "hangings" upon four pillars. Like the tabernacle and the inner veil, the "hangings" were also woven from four different colored fabrics. Lastly, we notice that the priests are only offering four types of creatures upon the Bronze Altar: the bullock, the lamb, the goat, and the turtledove. The number four pervades the journey from God's presence to man's realm of life – the same path the Son of God traveled to become the Son of Man.

The writer of Hebrews informs us that Christ's own flesh was a veil (Heb. 10:19-20). As stated above, coverings in Scripture reveal and conceal things. The Lord's flesh concealed the outshining glory of God but allowed His divine moral excellencies to be viewed by all. *"And the Word was made flesh, and dwelt among us, (and we beheld His glory, the glory as of the only begotten of the Father), full of grace and truth" (John 1:14).* The night before the Lord Jesus died we read of Him speaking to His disciples:

> *Jesus said to him, "Have I been with you so long, and yet you have not known Me, Philip? He who has seen Me has seen the Father; so how can you say, 'Show us the Father'? Do you not believe that I am in the Father, and the Father in Me? The words that I speak to you I do not speak on My own authority; but the Father who dwells in Me does the works. Believe Me that I am in the Father and the Father in Me, or else believe Me for the sake of the works themselves (John 14:9-11, NKJV).*

The veil of the Lord's flesh is pictured in the inner veil of the tabernacle. This veil hung upon four pillars; each pillar consisted of wood (speaking of Christ's humanity) overlaid with gold (declaring Christ's deity). God dwelt on one side of this veil and man on the other. What a depiction of the Messiah – He would be both God and man. He was both the Son of David and David's Lord (Mark 12:35-37).

As previously mentioned, the veil was woven with four colored fabrics, the basic four colors of all the coverings throughout the tabernacle. William MacDonald comments:

> The four colors of materials in the tabernacle with their symbolic meanings also seem to fit the evangelists' fourfold presentation of the attributes of our Lord!
>
> **Purple** is an obvious choice for Matthew, the Gospel of the King. Judges 8:26 shows the regal nature of this color.
>
> **Scarlet** dye was derived in ancient times from crushing a cochineal worm. This suggests Mark, the Gospel of the bondservant, *"a worm and no man" (Ps. 22:6).*
>
> **White** speaks of the righteous deeds of the saints (Rev. 19:8). Luke stresses the perfect humanity of Christ.
>
> **Blue** represents the sapphire dome we call the heavens (Ex. 24:10), an attractive representation of the Deity of Christ, a keynote in John.[5]

Why four Gospels? The Father provided perfect representation of His Son through four unique vantage points of His greatness. *Four* is the number pertaining to earthly order. It is the best number to declare the "good news" message – the goodness of God to mankind. The Son willingly laid aside His outshining glory and departed from His celestial home. He became subject to creation order and took the place upon an accursed tree for every man, woman and child that would ever live. There, rejected and abandoned, the billows and waves of divine judgement broke upon the Saviour as every human sin was judicially accounted for. Every lie, every evil thought, every immoral act, every murder, all unrighteousness was judged by God. After the judgment was complete, the Lord committed His spirit to His Father and died. He was laid in a borrowed tomb, and on the third day, as a testimony to the Father's complete satisfaction with the work at Calvary, the Son was raised up for our justification.

In Christ, we have eternal life, apart from Him there is no life – only death (separation from God). He now sits at the right hand of God and awaits that moment in time when He will return to the air to snatch away His bride from the earth. He will then restore rebellious Israel to God and establish His rightful eternal throne. The believer will co-inherit all things in Christ and co-reign with Christ forever. The Bible is really the only book of which it truly can be said that "they lived happily ever after." The Gospel of Jesus Christ, from every viewpoint, is "good news" indeed!

O Lord, when we the path retrace which Thou on earth hast trod,
To man Thy wondrous love and grace, Thy faithfulness to God;
Thy love, by man so sorely tried, proved stronger than the grave;
The very spear that pierced Thy side, drew forth the blood to save;
Unmoved by Satan's subtle wiles, or suffering, shame and loss,
Thy path, uncheered by earthly smiles, led only to the cross,
We wonder at Thy lowly mind, and fain would like Thee be,
And all our rest and pleasure find in learning, Lord of Thee.

– James Deck

# The Gospel of Matthew

# "Behold Your King"

*Rejoice greatly, O daughter of Zion! Shout, O daughter of Jerusalem!* **Behold, your King** *is coming to you; He is just and having salvation, lowly and riding on a donkey, A colt, the foal of a donkey (Zech. 9:9, NKJV).*

# Why is Matthew First?

The Hebrew Bible, the Old Testament in the complete canon of Scripture, is composed of twenty-five books. Since the Old Testament contains thirty-nine books, one might ask, "What is different?" The answer is that the content is the same, but the order and the names of the books vary somewhat, as do the books that are collected together into one title. In the Hebrew Bible, 1 and 2 Samuel is Samuel; 1 and 2 Kings is Kings; and 1 and 2 Chronicles is again, just the content of Chronicles. The last twelve books of the Old Testament, which we refer to as the "Minor Prophets," are all contained within one book in the Hebrew Bible entitled "The Minor Prophets." This expansion difference explains how we derive a thirty-nine book Old Testament from the Hebrew Bible's twenty-five book arrangement $(39 - 3 - 11 = 25)$.

The last book in the Hebrew Bible is **Chronicles**, so named by Jerome in his Latin translation; however, the Jews refer to Chronicles as "The Words of Days." The Jews commonly attribute the authorship of Chronicles to Ezra the scribe and, thus, would place its writing during the latter portion of the Babylonian/Persian captivity. It is noted that the first two verses in the book of Ezra are the same as the last two verses of 2 Chronicles, which provides some credence for the authorship of Ezra. Just as the Gospels tell the same story from different perspectives, Ezra (assuming he is the author) retells the story of David in Chronicles from a different vantage point than does the book of Samuel, which presents the plain historical account, including failures and their consequences as part of the record.

Though the content of 1 Chronicles and 2 Samuel is much the same, the "flavor" is different. Ezra's focus was to awaken a small, struggling community of exiled Jews to their heritage in Jehovah. They had lost their perspective of being God's covenant people, His chosen people on earth. They were a unique and distinctive people upon the earth and should have been elated by that reality. Chronicles calls the Jews into remembrance of the Levitical priesthood, which represented them to God, and the glorious kingdoms of David, Solomon and others. Within 1 Chronicles 1-8, Ezra provides the historical means of connecting this discouraged people to the beginning of their nation – through extensive genealogies, *"so all Israel were reckoned by genealogies" (1 Chron. 9:1).*

Why is Matthew the first book of the New Testament? The opening sentence both introduces the theme of Matthew and answers this question: *"The book of the generation of Jesus Christ, the Son of David, the Son of Abraham."* The principal topic is the direct fulfillment of the Davidic and Abrahamic covenants through Christ. These were unilateral covenants that God had made with David and Abraham but never had been completely fulfilled. For the Jews, the hope of permanent royalty from a man *"after God's own heart"* and the acquisition of the promissory blessing originally committed to *"the friend of God"* were paramount.

The genealogies of Matthew 1 served as proof to the Jews that Jesus, through Joseph, was a direct descendant of David and, thus, the legal and rightful heir to David's throne. As to not distract from his theme of covenant fulfillment, Matthew begins with Abraham, not Adam, in rendering Christ's genealogy. Luke's genealogy of Christ, however, is for a different purpose. Luke upholds Christ as the *"Son of man,"* or more specifically, the *"Son of Adam."* In so doing, Luke shows Christ to be the "Last Adam," God's replacement representative of righteousness and the literal fulfillment of the prophesied Messiah being derived from the *"seed of a woman" (Gen. 3:15-16)*. God thought it critical for mankind to understand that the Messiah would not be of the seed of fallen man, yet His royal lineage would be established through a man, Joseph, back to Solomon and finally David. The two genealogies accomplish this: Luke focuses our attention upon the Lord's humanity derived from Mary through the power of the Holy Spirit, while Matthew demonstrates Christ's official authority through Joseph.

The Hebrew Bible concludes with genealogies from Adam to the point in time in which God invoked 400 years of silence concerning His rebellious covenant people. This prophetic hush was broken with the announcement of the Saviour's coming to earth. In Matthew 1, the genealogies pick up again after the centuries of silence and lead the Jews to their much-anticipated and predicted Messiah, the Lord Jesus Christ. He would be the literal fulfillment of God's promise to David. God said, *"I will establish the throne of His kingdom forever" (2 Sam. 7:13)*. Matthew provides the culmination of the story, which Chronicles only partially disclosed, and bridges the remaining gap between the first Adam and the last Adam, who would restore righteousness and rule forever.

Clearly, God's covenant with Abraham had not been completely fulfilled, for the Jews were under brutal Gentile rule and were clearly not the esteemed people of the earth. Secondly, they have never possessed, at any time during their entire history, more than ten percent of the land promised to Abraham by God in Genesis 15 (Note: Joshua 21:43, refers to all the land to be possessed at that time.). Through Christ, the

Abrahamic covenant would be fulfilled. Listen to the prophetic words of Zacharias, the father of John the Baptist:

> Blessed is the Lord God of Israel, for He has visited and redeemed His people, and has raised up a horn of salvation for us in the house of His servant David, as He spoke by the mouth of His holy prophets, who have been since the world began, that we should be saved from our enemies and from the hand of all who hate us, to perform the mercy promised to our fathers and **to remember His holy covenant, the oath which He swore to our father Abraham**: To grant us that we, being delivered from the hand of our enemies, might serve Him without fear, in holiness and righteousness before Him all the days of our life *(Luke 1:68-75, NKJV)*.

The order of mention in the first verse of Matthew is important: the *"Son of David,"* then *"the Son of Abraham."* Normally, when these two chief patriarchs of the Jewish history are mentioned, Abraham is referred to first, for he walked upon the earth more than a thousand years before David was born. The order arranged by Matthew, however, introduces us to the "authority" theme of his Gospel. Who better than a Jewish official, a tax collector, to address the official glory of the Lord Jesus as rightful heir to the throne of David. The *"son of David"* refers specifically to the office of king. The Lord Jesus is the king of the Jews, but more than that, He is the King of kings and the Lord of lords (1 Tim. 6:15). He simply has not yet advanced to the earth to establish His throne; presently He resides upon His Father's throne in heaven (Rev. 3:21).

The reference to the *"son of Abraham"* is of a much wider scope than the reference to the *"son of David."* Through the son of Abraham *"shall all families of the earth be blessed"* *(Gen. 12:3)*. Paul speaks of Abraham as the spiritual father of all spiritual seed and of the eternal blessings which God promised to Abraham that are likewise offered to all those, who like Abraham, would simply believe God's word (Rom. 4:13-16). This is God's means of saving souls throughout all human history, whether Old Testament or New Testament. There may be varying messages of repentance and obedience to heed, but justification only occurs by grace through faith in what God proclaims is our responsibility. Only by faith can the work of Christ be accredited to our personal account.

> *For if Abraham was justified by works, he has something to boast about, but not before God. For what does the Scripture say? "Abraham believed God, and it was accounted to him for righteousness." Now to him who works, the wages are not counted as grace but as debt. But to him who does not work but believes on Him who justifies the ungodly, his faith is accounted for righteousness (Rom. 4:2-5 NKJV).*

If we want to work for our salvation, God is faithful to pay a fair wage; however, *"the wages of sin is death, but the gift of God is eternal life through Jesus Christ our Lord" (Rom. 6:23)*. It may not seem logical, but God just wants us to recognize that we can't save ourselves and that we must accept His free gift of salvation as the only means to be reconciled with Him. Oswald Chambers once said, "Faith is deliberate confidence in the character of God whose ways you cannot understand at the time."[1] Man's lingering guilt provokes him to do something to earn God's favor, but God is unimpressed with such attempts. The Gospel message candidly proclaims, "you can't *do* anything to be accepted by God: it's all been accomplished in Christ – you must only believe." Faith is a living trust in God, which ascends beyond what the five senses or human reasoning or intellectual arguments can verify.

This was Abraham's faith. He did not know **where** he was going, but at the call of God, he left Ur and went. He did not know **how** he would have natural children but reckoned the promise true. He did not know **why** he was to offer his only son Isaac but knew that God would have to raise him up if he struck him dead, for God's promises were in Isaac, and God is faithful to His word. He did not trust in his good deeds to earn God's favor. He did not give ear to human traditions that undermine God's word or to vain church rituals that offer salvation, for these make mockery of Christ's sacrifice. *"But without faith it is impossible to please Him: for he that cometh to God must believe that He is, and that He is a rewarder of them that diligently seek Him" (Heb. 11:6).*

In Christ, we see the very best aspects of both Jewish patriarchs. As the Son of David, Christ was the righteous king and a man after God's own heart, and as the Son of Abraham, He was a friend of God and a great man of faith – He lived to do the Father's will (John 6:38).

Matthew upholds the official glory of Christ as King; this is the prevalent theme of his testimony. Ten times he refers to Christ as the *"Son of David."* This is in contrast to the Gospel themes of Mark, Luke and John, which when combined, contain only five references to the Lord Jesus being the Son of David. It is, thus, properly placed first among the Gospels and first in the canonized New Testament. The Lord Jesus is the fullness and the fulfillment of the Old Testament covenants. *"For all the promises of God in Him are yea, and in Him Amen, unto the glory of God by us" (2 Cor. 1:20).* The Lord Jesus is the rightful heir to the throne of David and will deliver the Jews from all oppression, then rule over them in righteousness and peace forever.

# The Nobility of Matthew

When Christ walked upon the earth, the Jews had been without their own king for more than six centuries. Four different Gentile empires had ruled over them during that time; most of them cruelly. The Jews longed to be liberated from Roman oppression and to be a self-governing nation again. From this political ideology, the prophesied Messiah was coveted, but from a spiritual sense, the heart of the people had drifted far from God over the centuries of exile and silence. The *"feasts of Jehovah"* had become the *"feasts of the Jews."* The legalistic traditions of the Pharisees controlled the people harshly and perverted the clear teachings of the Mosaic Law. Their oral laws had declared it wrong to serve others or to do good deeds on the Sabbath day and upheld that it was more honorable to give money to God than to use it for the proper care of aged parents. So, when their long-awaited Messiah did arrive, His message of repentance and spiritual transformation were not only unwelcome but flatly rejected – it was not what the Jews wanted, but it was exactly what they needed.

## Outline

Often Scripture provides its own outline of a particular passage or book. For example, Revelation 1:19 provides a three-section outline for the entire book: *"Write the things which thou hast seen, and the things which are, and the things which shall be hereafter" (Rev. 1:19).* The phrase *"after these things"* in Genesis 15:1 and 22:1 also affords a threefold division of the life of Abraham (God's public, private, and prophetic dealings with His servant). The phrase *"from that time,"* found only twice in Matthew's Gospel (4:17 and 16:21), properly divides the book into three main sections:

> *"**From that time** ... Repent for the Kingdom of heaven is at hand" (Matt. 4:17).*
> *"**From that time** forth began Jesus to show unto His disciples, how that He must...suffer" (Matt. 16:21).*

Matthew 1:1 – 4:16   = Introduction
Matthew 4:17 – 16:20 = Presentation of the Jewish Messiah
Matthew 16:21– 28:20 = Rejection of the Jewish Messiah

The first section of Matthew informs us of the events leading up to the Lord's public ministry, which was initiated directly after His baptism and testing. The second section presents Messiah to the Jewish nation. The final portion of Matthew vividly describes the Messiah's rejection. This section commences after Peter's confession of Jesus, *"Thou art the Christ, the Son of the living God,"* and just prior to the Lord's transfiguration. It is within this portion of text that Matthew first records the Lord Jesus informing His disciples of His future suffering, death and resurrection.

The bulk of Matthew (the latter two sections) records the three-year-plus ministry of the Lord Jesus. Generally speaking, He labored in Galilee for approximately two years, then in Decapolis for six months and in Judea for three months, then withdrew to Perea for the final four months, prior to returning to Jerusalem for the Passover and crucifixion. The transfiguration of our Lord occurred in the later days of the

Decapolis ministry; thus, Matthew 4:17-16:20 covers nearly two and one-half years of history, while the last section in Matthew (16:21-28:20) spans the final seven or eight months of the Lord's sojourn on earth.

## Prophecies Concerning Christ

Matthew labors in his Gospel account to validate Jesus Christ as the Jewish Messiah – He was born of the Jews and for the Jews. He does so by frequently referring to Old Testament quotations and messianic prophecies, then shows that Jesus Christ is the literal fulfillment of each one. Consequently, his Gospel is strongly Jewish flavored. Where John repeatedly connects Christ to the completion of Old Testament "types," Matthew meticulously demonstrates that Christ is the culmination of Old Testament prophecies, or as John would later write, *"For the testimony of Jesus is the spirit of prophecy" (Rev. 19:10).* Bible prophecy finds its center in the life and ministry of Jesus Christ.

Because Matthew directly relates Jesus Christ to Old Testament declarations, the word "fulfilled" appears sixteen times in his Gospel. Fourteen of these references are clearly messianic, compared to eight in Mark, Luke, and John combined. It is noted that well over one hundred first advent prophecies concerning the Messiah are found in the Old Testament and that Jesus Christ fulfilled them all. The statistical probability of such a feat is astronomically impossible, but not for God's chosen Son.

The authority theme of Matthew is quite obvious in Christ's preaching and parable telling. How did the Lord commence His public ministry? John the Baptist had been preaching to the Jews: *"Repent ye, for the Kingdom of heaven is at hand" (Matt. 3:2).* Although Herod silenced John by incarceration, he could not thwart the Messiah from taking up John's message.

41

Matthew records the Lord's first words of public ministry: *"From that time Jesus began to preach, and to say, 'Repent, for the kingdom of heaven is at hand'" (Matt. 4:17).*

The Lord Jesus was the literal fulfillment of the kingdom message John had been proclaiming. John *"was a burning and a shining light" (John 5:35),* but his brilliance was destined to be quenched as soon as the *"Light of the World" (John 8:12)* showed forth His illumination. With John in prison, the King of the Jews began to directly call His subjects to repentance, which meant they needed to acknowledge Him as the sinless Messiah and their rightful King.

The same authority theme is prevalent in many of the parables Christ told. For example, in the parable of *The Marriage Feast,* Luke refers to the prominent character as *"a certain man" (Luke 14:16),* whereas Matthew is more specific with regard to his theme, *"a certain King" (Matt. 22:2).* Both accounts were accurate but different. Matthew upholds the kingly assertion in his Gospel, while Luke is careful not to distract from the humanity of Christ and the social appeal of the Saviour.

In the first two chapters alone, Matthew refers to Christ fulfilling five Old Testament prophecies relating to His birth and childhood.

> *Therefore the Lord himself shall give you a sign; Behold, a virgin shall conceive, and bear a son, and shall call his name Immanuel (Isa. 7:14).* **Jesus was born of a virgin.**

> *But thou, Bethlehem Ephratah, though thou be little among the thousands of Judah, yet out of thee shall he come forth unto me that is to be ruler in Israel; whose*

*goings forth have been from of old, from everlasting (Mic. 5:2).* **Jesus was born in Bethlehem.**

*When Israel was a child, then I loved him, and called my son out of Egypt (Hos. 11:1).* **Jesus lived in Egypt to escape Herod's wrath.**

*Thus saith the LORD; A voice was heard in Ramah, lamentation, and bitter weeping; Rachel weeping for her children refused to be comforted for her children, because they were not (Jer. 31:15).* **Herod murdered the baby boys of Ramah in an attempt to kill Jesus.**

*And there shall come forth a rod* [*netzer* – Nazarene] *out of the stem of Jesse, and a Branch shall grow out of his roots (Isa. 11:1).* **Jesus would live in Nazareth.**

# Dispensational

As there is some confusion to what the word "dispensation" actually means, a moment to clarify is needful. A dispensation is not a period of time, though dispensations advance within time. Dispensations are God's differing administrations among mankind. God reveals certain truths, spiritual economies if you will, for man to abide by. A dispensation works in time, but is not constrained by time. In fact, time proves or disproves man as being a faithful steward of the revelation God has entrusted to him. When man falters, God is just in rendering judgment. Throughout biblical history, God has revealed distinct administrations of order, dispensations, to meticulously demonstrate that, when given divine rules to live by, man will eventually go his own way and rebel against God. The purpose of these revealed economies is to show man his depraved heart (Rom. 3:20) and to prompt man to trust in God solely for his salvation (Gal. 3:24). L. Laurenson observes that the construction of Scripture relates directly to dispensations:

> The Bible is a book in two parts. The Old Testament has to do with the earth. It is the mind of Heaven revealed to man upon the earth to fit him for the earth. But man closed his ears to the voice of God, disobeyed the divine will, and made himself unfit for the earth in which God had placed him. Eden and innocence were lost by Adam. Canaan and liberty were lost by Israel. Happiness and holiness have been lost by all because of sin and disobedience. Hence the New Testament has to do with heaven. It reveals the mind of God as to how men, who had made themselves unfit for the earth, might be made fit for heaven itself through the Gospel.[1]

In Matthew, God is still dealing with Israel as before, on the ground of responsibility (as men upon the earth). Messiah had come. Would they accept or reject Him? The Kingdom Message itself was the culmination of a Jewish dispensational economy that began on Mount Sinai – the giving of the Law to Moses – and would conclude at Mount Moriah – the crucifixion of Christ. Fifty days later, the dispensation of the Church began, and both the message and the recipient of the message changed.

Matthew, more prominently than the other Gospel writers, shows the offering of Messiah, the Jewish rejection, and the consequential setting aside of Israel that the Gentiles might receive grace. *"Jesus Christ was a minister of the circumcision for the truth of God, to confirm the promises made unto the fathers; and that the Gentiles might glorify God for His mercy" (Rom. 15:8-9).* The Lord's ministry is mainly focused upon the *"lost sheep of the house of Israel,"* a term only found in Matthew (Matt. 10:6; 15:22-28). As long as Christ was on the earth preaching *"the kingdom of God has come,"* the disciples were instructed to only preach to the Jews – the kingdom Gospel was a specific message (a presentation of Messiah by words and signs) to the Jews.

Though the Jews rejected their Messiah and crucified Him, God is not done with the Jewish people. The whole of Romans 11 proclaims that God has always preserved a remnant of spiritually-minded Jews for His glory, and in a coming day, the very Gentiles who received an offer of grace because of the Jewish rejection will be the means in which God provokes Israel to jealousy. During the tribulation period, the Jewish Nation will turn back to God and receive their Messiah, the Lord Jesus (Joel 2; Zech. 12; and Ezek. 36 and 37).

Matthew highlighted the forthcoming dispensational change in the latter portion of his account. After Peter's statement of Jesus being the Christ, the Lord mentions the Church for the first time, then foretells of His sufferings in Jerusalem. Matthew is the only Gospel to reference the Church (Matt. 16:18; 18:17) and only after Israel's rejection of Christ. From this point on, Christ is less public in His ministry, though still upholding the message of the Kingdom until Messiah is cut off.

## Jewish Attitude

As stated above, the Jews were not looking for their Messiah in a true spiritual sense. This fact is clearly exemplified in the Jewish response to the eastern wise men and to the ministry of John the Baptist. Unexpectedly, foreign diplomats arrived in Jerusalem inquiring, *"Where is He that is born King of the Jews? For we have seen His star in the east, and are come to worship Him" (Matt. 2:2).* After the Jews had informed the magi that Bethlehem was to be the birthplace of the Messiah, did they accompany their foreign visitors to assist in searching out their prophesied king? No. Herod told the wise men to *"go and search diligently for the young child; and when ye have found Him, bring me word again, that I may come and worship Him also" (Matt. 2:8).* No eagerness to find God's foretold King of the Jews was evident among them; in fact, Herod later proved that his only reason for directing the magi as he did was so he could locate and murder any rival to his authority. The heart of the Jews was so far from Jehovah that they had no desire or love for His Messiah.

Being warned in a dream, Joseph removed his young family to Egypt. Later, after the death of Herod the Great, Joseph returned his family to the land of Israel, but being again warned in a dream, he turned aside to live in Nazareth, for he feared Herod's son Archelaus. In a poetic sense, the Saviour, in those early years, retraced the very steps of Israel's infant history (Canaan to Egypt in distress, and back to Canaan after the enemy had been vanquished).

Notice that earthly kings were responsible for the early movements of the Lord Jesus. His original pilgrimage to Bethlehem in the womb of Mary resulted from the registration decreed by Caesar Augustus. The Lord's hurried departure to Egypt resulted from the evil act Herod sought to do against Him, and the Lord traveled to Nazareth because Joseph feared Archelaus. To demonstrate the sovereign power of God, the highest human authorities on earth worked to accomplish the foreordained counsel of God. Through the presence and administrations of these three kings, the Old Testament prophecies pertaining to Christ's birth, foreign travels, and hometown were all fulfilled.

## Kingdom of Heaven

The phrase *"kingdom of heaven"* is found thirty-two times in Matthew but nowhere else in all of Scripture. This peculiarity must be associated with the theme of his Gospel. The similar and associated term *"kingdom of God"* is applied fifty-four times in the Gospel accounts, but only appears five times in Matthew and merely twice in John. What is the significance of these phrases, and how do the two terms relate to each other?

Centuries of debate on this subject prove insufficient to answer this question fully. The terms are used interchangeably by the Lord during the Sermon on the Mount and the Lord's discussion with His disciples concerning the rich young ruler who valued his wealth above following the Lord (Matt. 19:23-24). These instances seem to indicate that there is minimal difference in the meaning of the terms, or perhaps, an interrelated meaning (one term being a subset of the other).

Some Bible scholars note a distinction in that the kingdom of heaven is a subset of the kingdom of God. The *"kingdom of heaven"* in this case refers to the realm of human profession in which one acknowledges the sovereign rule of God or *"the kingdom of God."* C. I. Scofield writes:

> The kingdom of heaven is similar in many respects to the kingdom of God and is often used synonymously with it, though emphasizing certain features of divine government. When contrasted with the universal kingdom of God, the kingdom of heaven includes only men on earth, excluding angels and other creatures. The kingdom of heaven is the earthly sphere of profession as shown by the inclusion of these designated as wheat and tares, the latter of which are cast out of the kingdom (Matt. 13:41), and is compared to a net containing both the good and bad fish which are later separated (Matt. 13:47).[2]

Other commentators, such as William MacDonald, acknowledge a realm of human profession within the kingdom of heaven, which is composed of true believers and mere professors, but sees no tangible disagreement between the terms *"kingdom of heaven"* and *"kingdom of God."* He writes:

The kingdom of heaven is the sphere in which God's rule is acknowledged. The word heaven is used figuratively to denote God; this is clearly shown in Daniel 4:25-26. In verse 25, Daniel said that the Most High rules in the kingdom of men. In the very next verse he says that Heaven rules. Thus the kingdom of heaven announces the rule of God, which exists wherever people submit to that rule.[3]

It is important to understand that *"kingdom of heaven"* and the church are not synonymous terms, for the kingdom of heaven contains both the children of God and the children of the devil, while the universal church is only composed of true believers. Those who have believed the Gospel message experience rebirth and become children of God (John 1:12-13; Eph. 2:1-6).

So, why is the term *"kingdom of heaven"* unique to Matthew? The Jews would have been familiar with the prophet Daniel's association of "heaven" and "kingdom" terminology in declaring the scene in which the Son of man (Christ) would return to earth from heaven to establish an everlasting dominion:

> *I saw in the night visions, and, behold, one like **the Son of man came with the clouds of heaven**, and came to the Ancient of days, and they brought Him near before Him. And there was given Him dominion, and glory, and **a kingdom**, that all people, nations, and languages, should serve Him: His dominion is an everlasting dominion, which shall not pass away, and **His kingdom** that which shall not be destroyed (Dan 7:13-14).*

Matthew's presentation of Jesus as the Jewish Messiah and Daniel's foretelling of Messiah coming from heaven to establish rightful authority over the Jews, combine nicely to speak of the *"kingdom of heaven"* message (or offer, if you will). Would the Jews acknowledge His claim of authority over them? The term *"kingdom of heaven"* seems to relate to the presentation of Christ and the decision of the people to accept or reject Him as king. L. Laurenson summarizes the matter:

> The expression "Kingdom of Heaven" is found only in Matthew; and only in Matthew do we get the "Gospel of the Kingdom," and that thrice repeated (Chapters 4, 9, 24). Here was the cure for all the ills that afflicted Jehovah's land; but, alas! Israel refused the Gospel of the Kingdom then, as sinners today refuse the Gospel of Grace. And there never was grace like the grace of Christ.[4]

## Son of David

As mentioned in the introduction, the phrase *"son of David"* occurs ten times in Matthew but only three times each in Mark and Luke. The phrase *"son of David"* is not to be found in John, for that would only undermine the presentation of Jesus Christ as the Son of God. The son of David refers specifically to the Lord's official glory as king and to His position as the rightful heir to the throne of David. After the Lord cast a demon out of a boy to heal his dumbness, Luke recorded that *"the people wondered" (Luke 11:14),* but Matthew, describing the same miracle, wrote, *"and all the people were amazed, and said, Is not this the son of David" (Matt. 12:23).* Matthew was compelled to emphasize the title *"son of David"* whereas Luke received no prompting of the Holy Spirit to do so.

## The Temptation (Testing) of Christ

If the accounts of Matthew 4 and Luke 4 are examined closely, one will notice that the order of Satan's specific attacks upon Christ are different. The skeptic deplores such inconsistency: "See you can't trust the Bible – it does not agree with itself."

However, the order maintained by each writer is for the purpose of upholding the prevalent theme of each Gospel. In Matthew, Satan first asks the Lord Jesus to turn the stones into bread, then bids Him to cast Himself down from the pinnacle of the temple, and thirdly offers to Christ all the kingdoms of this world, if Christ will only worship him. Luke's order, however, is first the request to turn the stones into bread, then the offer of the kingdoms of the world, and finally Satan adjures Christ to cast Himself down from the pinnacle of the temple to prove that the angels will protect Him. Why the different order? Arthur Pink explains:

> The reason for this variation is not hard to find. In Matthew, the order is arranged climactically, so as to make Rulership over all the kingdoms of the world the final bait which the Devil dangled before the Son of David. But in Luke we have, no doubt, the chronological order, the order in which they actually occurred, and these correspond with the order of temptation of the first man and his wife in Eden, where the appeal was made, as here in Luke, to the lust of the flesh, the lust of the eyes, and the pride of life (see 1 Jn. 2:16 and compare Gen. 3:6).[5]

Sovereign design accounts for the variation of the temptation accounts, which serves to further declare the wisdom of God and the distinct glories of the Son. Luke's order of temptations is chronological, while Matthew arranged it climactically unto kingship.

## Miracles

Paul acknowledges the natural propensity of the Jewish people to be guided by sight rather than faith, *"For the Jews require a sign, and the Greeks seek after wisdom"* (1 Cor. 1:22). The Lord Jesus said, *"this is an evil generation, they seek a sign"* (Luke 11:29). The Lord performed ample miracles while on earth, yet the Jews did not believe that He was the Messiah and, in fact, crucified Him. Peter determinedly proclaimed this point at Pentecost (the first day of the Church Age):

*Ye men of Israel, hear these words; Jesus of Nazareth, a **man approved of God among you by miracles and wonders and signs**, which God did by Him in the midst of you, as ye yourselves also know: Him, being delivered by the determinate counsel and foreknowledge of God, ye have taken, and by wicked hands have crucified and slain: Whom God hath raised up, having loosed the pains of death: because it was not possible that He should be holden of it (Acts 2:22-24).*

The word "miracle" is not found in Matthew's Gospel; rather, the miracles that the Lord performed are referred to as "signs." Signs of what? The signs witnessed by Israel were irrefutable evidence proving that Christ was who He claimed to be – the Messiah. The Lord's preaching and signs composed the kingdom message to the Jews; Arthur Pink explains:

Our Lord's miracles of healing were not simply exhibitions of power, or manifestations of mercy, they were also a supplement to His preaching and teaching, and their prime value was **evidential**. These miracles, which are frequently termed "signs," formed an essential part of Messiah's credentials. This is established, unequivocally, by what we read of in Matthew 11. When John the Baptist was cast into prison, his faith as to the Messiahship of Jesus wavered, and so he sent two of His disciples unto Him, asking, *"Art thou He that should come or do we look for another?" (Matt. 11:3)*. Notice, carefully, the Lord's reply, *"Go and show John again those things which ye do **hear and see**: The blind receive their sight, and the lame walk, the lepers are* *cleansed, and the deaf hear, the dead are raised up, and the poor have the Gospel preached to them" (Matt. 11:4-5).*

Appeal was made to two things: His teaching and His miracles of healing. The two are linked together, again, in Matthew 9:35 – *"And Jesus went about all the cities and villages, teaching in their synagogues, and preaching the Gospel of the Kingdom, and healing every sickness, and every disease among the people."* And, again, when the Lord sent forth the Twelve, *"But go rather to the lost sheep of the House of Israel. And as ye go, preach, saying, The Kingdom of heaven is at hand. Heal the sick, raise the dead, cast out demons; freely ye have received, freely give" (Matt. 10:6-8).* Miracles of healing, then were integrally connected with the kingdom testimony. They are among the most important of "The **Signs** of the times" concerning which the Messiah reproached the Pharisees and Sadducees for their failure to discern (see Matt. 16:1-3). Similar miracles of healing shall be repeated when the Messiah returns to the earth (Isa. 35:4-6).[6]

Though the signs provided proof that Jesus was the Christ, they would prove insufficient to cause the people to trust the Messiah for salvation. *"Without faith it is impossible to please Him* [God]*" (Heb. 11:6),* and faith requires the soul to venture beyond what the senses can verify.

The Lord Jesus stated that it was the unrighteous who wanted to see a "sign or a wonder" in order to believe in Him. He called these "sign seekers" an evil generation (Matt. 12:38-39). Even those people who had witnessed the miracle of the feeding of the 5,000 were pestering the Lord the very next day: *"What sign showest Thou, then, that we **may see and believe Thee" (John 6:30)?*** Had they not recalled the miracle the day before? Did they not fill their bellies with a boy's multiplied sack lunch? The Israelites saw miracles every day in the wilderness for forty years, yet it did not increase their spirituality – for they constantly murmured against God and His leadership. This shallow spiritual mentality was clearly evident while the Lord Jesus was hanging on the cross: *"Let Christ the King of Israel descend now from the cross, that we **may see and believe**..." (Mark 15:32).*

Peter shows us that true spiritual faith opens our eyes to understand the spiritual things of God. When the Lord asked His twelve disciples if they, too, would turn away from Him, as many had done, Peter responded, *"Lord to whom shall we go? Thou hast the words of eternal life. And we **believe and are sure** that Thou art that Christ, the Son of the living God" (John 6:68-69).* The unrighteous want a sign to believe, but the righteous believe, then understand. Thus, until we exercise faith, we will not understand from where we came and to where we journey. *"Through faith we understand that the worlds were framed by the Word of God, so that things which are seen were not made of things which do appear" (Heb. 11:3).* Oswald Chambers summarizes the matter of believing and understanding this way: "I must know Jesus Christ as Saviour before His teaching has any meaning for me other than that of an ideal which leads to despair."[7]

Though the Lord knew that the Jews would not believe in Him through signs alone, He understood the need to fulfill Scripture and work wonders before them. The miracles served to establish the Messiah's credentials; therefore, the Lord referred to the signs He had performed to prove He was the Messiah: *"But I have greater witness than that of John: for the works which the Father hath given Me to finish, the same works that I do, bear witness of Me, that the Father hath sent Me" (John 5:36).* To the non-believers He pleaded, *"If I do not the works of My Father, believe Me not. But if I do, though ye believe not Me, believe the works: that ye may know, and believe, that the Father is in Me, and I in Him" (John 10:37-38).*

## Sermon on the Mount

The Sermon on the Mount is the manifesto of the King, literally the kingdom's constitution. Matthew (chapters five through seven) documents the Lord's lengthy dissertation to His subjects, as Israel's yet to be enthroned King. Luke records a portion of a similar message (approximately thirty verses) given on a different day, while Mark and John do not mention it at all. The Sermon on the Mount, thus, strongly fits with Matthew's perspective of the Lord Jesus Christ. Even the Jews that listened to the Lord Jesus understood the tone of His exhortation, in which He would say fourteen times, *"I say unto you."* At the conclusion of the sermon, we read, *"the people were astonished at His doctrine: for He taught them as **One having authority**, and not as the scribes" (7:28-29).* The King spoke as the One in authority!

Within this lengthy discourse recorded in Matthew, the Lord addressed the ideal character and conduct of the subjects of His kingdom and what their circle of influence and testimony ought to be. Luke's focus pertains more to the lifestyle of the disciples in personal witnessing. For example: in Matthew, the Lord pronounced a blessing upon *"the poor in spirit" (M*att. 5:3); but in Luke the blessing is to *"the poor" (*Luke 6:20).

Much of the Lord's declaration conveyed a flat rejection of the traditions and practices of the Pharisees. In the closing, He told the people that they were now accountable for what they had heard: Would they follow Him and build their lives upon His teachings, or would they continue to follow empty religious traditions and human reasoning (i.e. building their house on a foundation of sand)? When the storms of life would come, the latter would prove to be a total "washout," while those who built upon His word (the rock) would stand fast and enjoy an abiding peace in life, despite difficulties.

The Sermon on the Mount will be the constitution of the millennial kingdom, once Christ returns to earth to establish it. Although it is true that those in the church age who have the Holy Spirit indwelling them should be exhibiting behavior consistent with the Kingdom Constitution, the kingdom exists now in only that spiritual sense. The literal sense is yet future. The Gospel message of the Kingdom was delivered to the Jewish people as an appeal to repent and receive Jesus Christ as Messiah and King. William MacDonald comments on this important distinction:

> While there is only one Gospel, there are different features of the Gospel in different times. For instance, there is a different emphasis between the Gospel of the kingdom and the Gospel of the grace of God. The Gospel of the kingdom says, "Repent and receive the Messiah, then you will enter His kingdom when it is set up on earth." The Gospel of grace says, "Repent and receive Christ; then you will be taken up to meet Him and to be with Him forever." Fundamentally, they are the same Gospel – salvation by grace through faith – but they show that there are different administrations of the Gospel according to God's dispensational purposes.
>
> When Jesus preached the Gospel of the kingdom, He was announcing His coming as King of the Jews and explaining the terms of admission into His kingdom. His miracles showed the wholesome nature of the kingdom.[8]

The "Gospel of the Kingdom" and the "Gospel of Grace" preached now in the church age are both founded in God's grace and both require personal faith to appropriate God's blessing, but each has a distinct message, beneficiary, and dispensational focus.

Arthur Pink notes the dispensational distinction of the Gospel message:

> *"And Jesus went about all Galilee teaching in their synagogues, and preaching the Gospel* (not, be it noted, the "Gospel of the Grace of God" – Acts 20:24; nor "the Gospel of Peace" – Eph. 6:15; but "the Gospel") *of the Kingdom, and healing all manner of sickness and all manner of disease among the people" (Matt. 4:23).*[9]

To not draw distinction between the Gospel message of the Kingdom, preached by Christ to the "Lost House of Israel," and the Gospel of Grace, preached presently during the Church Age, will result in doctrinal error. The Gospel commanded to be preached now was not publicly proclaimed during Christ's ministry on earth, for if Satan had known what God was accomplishing through Christ, the princes of the world *would have not crucified the Lord of glory (1 Cor. 2:7-8).* Of course the sufferings of Christ were predetermined by the counsel of God before the foundation of the world (1 Pet. 1:19-20) – thus God, not Satan, is responsible for Calvary.

Furthermore, the Lord Jesus visited Paul personally to convey to him exactly what the Gospel message during the Church age would be:

> *Moreover, brethren, I declare unto you the Gospel which I preached unto you, which also ye have received, and wherein ye stand; by which also ye are saved, if ye keep in memory what I preached unto you, unless ye have believed in vain. For I delivered unto you first of all that which I also received, how that Christ died for our sins according to the scriptures; and that he was buried, and that he rose again the third day according to the scriptures (1 Cor. 15:1-4,* also see Gal. 1:6-12).

Spiritual application within the Sermon on the Mount for believers today will certainly be gleaned, but the literal intent of the message was for Israel. The hope of the Jew is to see their Messiah reigning on earth and to be nationally restored with God, as His covenant people. The hope of the church will conclude prior to this literal fulfillment, when the Lord Jesus descends to the clouds and "catches up" the church to be with Him in heaven (1 Thess. 4:13-18; 1 Cor. 15:51-52). The Church has a heavenly hope; the Jews have an earthly promise. When the Christian beholds Christ face to face in a glorified body, faith and hope will have served their purpose, but love will endure forever (1 Cor. 13:8).

## The Olivet Discourse

The Tuesday three days prior to the Lord's death was an incredibly busy day for the Lord Jesus. Besides mastering the verbal challenges of the Herodians, the Sadducees, the Pharisees, the Scribes, and a lawyer, He also spoke the "Woe" message to the Pharisees and conveyed several parables. After these events, the Lord departed with His disciples to the Mount of Olives for a time of private ministry. At this time, He proclaimed to them important details concerning the future of Israel and the time of His Second Advent to the earth. Because this teaching was private and on the Mount of Olives, it is often referred to as "The Olivet Discourse." As with the "Sermon on the Mount," Matthew records the specific details more prominently than the other evangelists (Matt. 24-25). Both Mark and Luke devote one chapter each to the narration (Mark 13 and Luke 21), while John does not mention the discourse at all. Much of the detail contained in Matthew 25 is completely unique to Matthew.

The Olivet Discourse again is **strictly** Jewish, for the Church will already be in heaven before the events of the

Tribulation Period begin to unfold. The Olivet Discourse provides escalating signs of the coming Tribulation Period and describes events in the first half, mid, and last half of this horrendous time on earth. Then the Lord spoke of His Second Coming to the earth to judge the wicked. Only in Matthew do we read the words: *"Then shall the King say unto them on His right hand, come, ye blessed of My Father, inherit the kingdom..." (Matt. 25:34). "And the King shall answer and say... unto them on the left hand, Depart from me, ye cursed, into everlasting fire..." (Matt. 25:40-41).* The message resounds with a theme of watchfulness throughout – the Jews should not be deceived by the forthcoming Anti-Christ but should instead wait for the Lord Jesus to return to judge the wicked and to establish His kingdom. *"Watch, therefore; for ye know not what hour your Lord doth come" (Matt. 24:42).*

## The Number Two

Under the Mosaic Law, at least two witnesses were required to substantiate a legal claim or allegation (Deut. 19:15). While offering instructions in how to reconcile an offense with a brother, the Lord acknowledged the importance of two witnesses to confirm the truth. *"But if he will not hear thee, then take with thee one or two more, **that in the mouth of two or three witnesses every word may be established"** (Matt. 18:16).* Matthew is the only Gospel writer to record these statements of the Lord Jesus.

As Matthew is mainly addressing a Jewish audience, he is conscious of this legal regulation in his writing. Though the other Gospel writers neglect this detail, he often identifies the existence of **two** witnesses to legally substantiate important events of the Lord's life.

Matthew records that there were:

**two** demon-possessed individuals cured by Christ in the country of the Gergesenes (Matt. 8:28),

**two** blind men healed by Christ near Nazareth (Matt. 9:27),

**two** of John's disciples who came to inquire of Jesus (Matt. 11:2),

**two** blind men healed by Christ leaving Jericho (Matt. 20:30); one was Bartimaeus (Mark 10:46),

**two** false witnesses at His trial (Matt. 26:60),

**two** Gentile witnesses of nobility attesting to His innocence (Both Pilate and his wife declared Christ was a righteous man – Matt. 27:19, 24.).

Matthew's focus on **two** witnesses is unique, for none of the other Gospel writers were compelled by the Holy Spirit to record the above details.

## Mountains

Symbolically speaking, mountains refer to "kingdoms" in Scripture. Daniel invokes this imagery to speak of the Lord Jesus coming into His kingdom after all Gentile powers had been judged (Dan. 2:44-45). John applies the metaphorical meaning in Revelation 17 where seven mountains are described as seven kingdoms. Matthew, upholding the nobility of Christ, references mountains to signify His forthcoming earthly kingdom. Though all the Gospels record the Lord venturing up and down mountains during His ministry, the other writers, for the most part, do not apply the symbolic representation during key events as Matthew does (In some cases the events are recorded without reference to a mountain.). Examples include:

Sermon on the Mount (Matt. 5-7): No mention in the other Gospels.

Transfiguration (High Mount – Matt. 17:1): No mention in John.
Olivet Discourse (Matt. 24:3): No mention in Luke or John.
Galilee Commission (Matt. 28:16): No mention in the other Gospels.

# Angels

Angels are rarely mentioned in Mark and John, but Matthew and Luke refer to them 43 times, yet from different viewpoints. In general, Matthew refers to these spiritual beings as messengers of God (mainly communicating through dreams) and as subordinates doing the Lord's bidding. Luke emphasizes their various ministries, including praising God, being His messengers and being witnesses to His earthly operations. Perhaps Mark does not refer much to the ministry of angels because the ministry of the humble Servant of Jehovah is primary. In John, the Lord Jesus, the Supreme Son of God, is entrusted with all the work; no one else, not even the disciples, share in the Lord's ministry. The authority theme of Matthew is upheld in the Lord's relationship with the angels, as He often commands their activities.

*The Son of man shall send forth His angels, and they shall gather out of His kingdom all things that offend, and them which do iniquity (Matt. 13:41).*

*For the Son of man shall come in the glory of His Father with His angels; and then He shall reward every man according to His works (Matt. 16:27).*

*And He shall send His angels with a great sound of a trumpet, and they shall gather together His elect from the four winds, from one end of heaven to the other (Matt. 24:31).*

*When the Son of man shall come in His glory, and all the holy angels with Him, then shall He sit upon the throne of His glory (Matt. 25:31).*

*Thinkest thou that I cannot now pray to My Father, and He shall presently give Me more than twelve legions of angels (Matt. 26:53).*

Luke is the only Gospel writer to record that an angel assisted the Lord in the Garden of Gethsemane. The purpose of this visit was to "strengthen" the Lord. Contemplating Calvary had agitated the Lord's soul, but an entire night of prayer had quieted His heart, though it left Him physically and emotionally exhausted. Though the "strengthening" language is consistent with Luke's "Son of Man" theme, it would be out of place in Matthew. Once in Matthew, after the forty-day period in which Satan unsuccessfully solicited the Lord to sin, we read of angels "ministering" or "serving" the Lord. Compare these two passages in Luke and Matthew:

*Then saith Jesus unto him, Get thee hence, Satan: for it is written, Thou shalt worship the Lord thy God, and Him only shalt thou serve. Then the devil leaveth Him, and, behold, **angels came and ministered unto Him** (Matt. 4:11).*

*And there appeared **an angel** unto Him from heaven, **strengthening Him** (Luke 22:43).*

Only Matthew records the Lord Jesus rebuking and commanding Satan to go at the end of the forty days of testing. The word translated "ministered" in Matthew is *diakoneo*, which means "to be an attendant or wait upon." It is the same Greek word from which the church office of deacon is derived. Luke uses *enischuo*, which means "to invigorate or make strong" to describe the ministry of the angels to Christ. Luke draws our attention to the Lord's frail humanity to demonstrate that, like us, He also was prone to weariness, thirst, hunger, emotional distress, etc.

# Dreams

A comparison of the Gospel records reveals that the word "dream" only occurs in Matthew. It is found six times and is used exclusively to impart divine information, usually through an angelic means. In Matthew, divine revelation is provided in a less personal and less direct means than the angelic communications in Luke's record. In Luke, angels met face to face with individuals and personally conveyed the good tidings through normal interactive speech. This form of human communication fits well with Luke's perspective of Christ's humanity. In Matthew, the information is authoritative, unidirectional, to the point, and without any opportunity for the interpersonal dialogue.

# Worship

Matthew records ten different times in which the Lord Jesus received worship, compared to three worship events in Mark, one in Luke after Christ's resurrection, and one specifically stated act of worship in John by the healed blind man, although Mary's sacrificial devotion was unquestionably an act of reverence too. Mark and Luke chronicle many of the same events in which worship was bestowed upon the Lord in Matthew's record but without a specific reference to worship. As to not dilute the authoritative aroma of Matthew, Mark and Luke describe the act of worship rather than referring to worship itself. The following passages serve as examples:

### The Cleansed Leper
*And, behold, there came a leper and **worshipped Him**, saying, Lord, if Thou wilt, thou canst make me clean (Matt. 8:2).*

*And there came a leper to Him, beseeching Him, and **kneeling down to Him**, and saying unto Him, If thou wilt, thou canst make me clean (Mark 1:40).*

*And it came to pass, when He was in a certain city, behold a man full of leprosy: **who seeing Jesus fell on his face**, and besought Him, saying, Lord, if Thou wilt, thou canst make me clean (Luke 5:12).*

### Jairus
*While He spake these things unto them, behold, there came a certain ruler, and **worshipped Him**, saying, My daughter is even now dead: but come and lay thy hand upon her, and she shall live (Matt. 9:18).*

*And, behold, there cometh one of the rulers of the synagogue, Jairus by name; and when he saw Him, **he fell at His feet** (Mark 5:22).*

*And, behold, there came a man named Jairus, and he was a ruler of the synagogue: **and he fell down at Jesus' feet**, and besought Him that He would come into his house (Luke 8:41).*

### Syrophenician Woman
*Then came she and **worshipped Him**, saying, Lord, help me (Matt. 15:25).*

*For a certain woman, whose young daughter had an unclean spirit, heard of Him, and came and **fell at His feet** (Mark 7:25).*

# Hell
The King has authority to judge all unfaithful and rebellious subjects of His kingdom. Matthew expresses Christ's rightful authority to be judge through frequent references to the eternal punishment of the wicked in "hell." The King James Version of the Bible does not differentiate between the two Greek words, *genna* and *haides*, translated "hell." *Genna* refers to the location of continued rubbish burning, the valley of Hinnom just southwest of Jerusalem. It is used figuratively as a name for the

place of everlasting punishment. *Haides,* or Hades, speaks of the temporary realm in which unsaved departed souls await the Great White Throne judgment (Rev. 20:11-15). Hades, after giving up its souls for judgment, is cast into the Lake of Fire (Rev. 20:14). As to not get confused with semantics, we will refer to *Genna,* as "Hell" or as the "Eternal Lake of Fire."

| Term of Judgment | Matthew | Mark | Luke | John |
|------------------|---------|------|------|------|
| Hades | 2 | 0 | 2 | 0 |
| Hell | 7 | 3 | 1 | 0 |
| Everlasting Punishment | 1 | 0 | 0 | 0 |
| Everlasting Fire | 2 | 0 | 0 | 0 |
| **Total** | **12** | **3** | **3** | **0** |

There is a place called Hell in which Satan and his angels (Matt. 25:41) and all those who reject Christ (Matt. 11:23) will be eternally judged. Matthew clearly magnifies the judicial role of Christ. He is completely righteous in executing judgment of the wicked and able to do so.

## Righteousness

Matthew emphasizes God's righteousness in a way that substantiates mankind's inherent unrighteous state, humanity's need to be righteous, and man's natural propensity to boast of self-righteousness. Of the twenty-nine times that the words "righteous" or "righteousness" are found in the Gospels, nineteen reside in Matthew.

*Blessed are they which do hunger and thirst after righteousness... (Matt. 5:6).*

*Blessed are they which are persecuted for righteousness' sake... (Matt. 5:10).*

> *But seek ye first the kingdom of God, and His righteousness... (Matt. 6:33).*

> *I am not come to call the righteous, but sinners to repentance (Matt. 9:13).*

The subject of righteousness unquestionably relates to Christ's legitimate claim to the throne of David, from which He will establish an endless rule of righteousness. The kingdom manifesto in Matthew 5 demands righteous subjects for this kingdom, for Christ's kingdom will be thoroughly evidenced by the righteousness of God. By such association with Him, God's holy character demands dedicated and yielded subjects. *"Be ye holy for I am Holy"* (1 Pet. 1:16). *"Serve God acceptably with reverence and godly fear; for our God is a consuming fire"* (Heb. 12:28-29). The Jews rejected both Christ's righteousness and His call to righteousness and are, to this day, a suffering people waiting for their Messiah. The Jewish nation will readily acknowledge Jesus Christ as Messiah at His Second Advent (Zech. 12:10). Isaiah describes Messiah's ministry on earth at that time:

> *But with **righteousness** shall He judge the poor, and reprove with equity for the meek of the earth: and He shall smite the earth with the rod of His mouth, and with the breath of His lips shall he slay the wicked. And **righteousness** shall be the girdle of His loins, and faithfulness the girdle of His* [waist] *(Isa. 11:4-5).*

## Throne and Altars

Scripture often presents what seem to be unconnected and even contrasting subjects in tandem so that a fuller spiritual teaching might be offered than if these were separately. For example, God called upon **prophets** to represent Himself to the people but used **priests** to represent

65

the people to Himself. It may seem that Paul and James are in disagreement regarding how salvation is received, yet both apostles are merely two bookends on the whole truth: Man is saved by grace through faith, but faith never stands alone; it has to be evidenced by good works. Many have been confused concerning the two advents of Christ, but both are absolutely necessary. The purpose of Christ's first advent was to be a sacrifice for sin and to offer grace to whosoever will, but His second advent to the earth will be to judge the wicked, comfort the oppressed, and rule the world in righteousness.

Another topical pairing that proclaims a broader truth than they would if depicted individually is the **throne** and the **altar**. The word "throne" is found five times in the four Gospels; four of these occur in Matthew. Likewise, the word "altar" is rendered eight times altogether in the Gospels, with six of these references being in Matthew. What meaning is being conveyed through more frequent reference to **thrones and altars** in Matthew? Though the Old Testament contains several references to this association, two such examples will be adequate to demonstrate the general spiritual meaning.

Adonijah, who had aspired to be king, feared Solomon after their father David had seated Solomon on the throne. Adonijah fled to the Brazen Altar in the temple and while embracing the horns of the altar, Solomon granted him mercy; however, Solomon's mercy was contingent upon Adonijah continuing in well-doing. Later, the warning was not heeded, and Adonijah was judged (1 Kgs. 1:48–52). In this story, the throne, a symbol of authority, appears first, then after awareness of this authority, the altar was sought to obtain mercy.

Isaiah beheld the majestic glory of God's throne (Isa. 6:1-7). His response to the revealed holiness of God was *"Woe is to me, for I am undone."* At that moment, he was not mindful of what he had or had not done, nor of what he should have done, but of his spiritual position before Almighty God. When man stands before the throne of God, there is no excuse, nowhere to shift blame; outside of Christ, we all stand condemned: "I am a sinner, and I am guilty." But as soon as Isaiah acknowledged his condition before God, God's response was immediate and effectual. A seraph hovering about the throne of God swooped down and snatched a hot coal from off the altar and pressed it to Isaiah's lips to show God's ability to purify sinners. Through the altar, he received grace and found a holy standing before God.

Matthew's message to the Jewish nation is twofold – "the throne of Christ" and "the altar of Christ." Anyone acknowledging His divine righteousness will also be compelled to repent and embrace God's altar, the finished work of Christ at Calvary. This is why righteousness and repentance are so duly stressed in Matthew. The throne must be understood first, or the altar will have no meaning or benefit. Only when man understands his lost and unsaved state before God can he be found and saved by God. For those awakened to their depraved and destitute state, God's finger quickly points the way to restoration – the cross of Christ. As the writer of Hebrews proclaims, "We have an Altar," but it is completely outside Judaism and any system of human works and requires an individual to identify with Christ and, thus, bear His reproach (Heb. 13:10-13). Those who reject God's offer in Christ will be judged. Because the Jews rejected His throne and altar, Christ, from the Mount of Olives, wept over them and then foretold the devastating judgment that would come upon them.

## Key Words or Phrases

In the above observations, several key words and phrases have been distinguished. These serve as support beams in Matthew's overall framework of presenting Christ as the King of the Jews. The following key words or phrases are either peculiar to Matthew or more prominent in Matthew than in the other Gospel accounts: "king," "throne," "altar," "righteousness," "kingdom of heaven," "hell," "dream," "prophet," "fulfilled," "two," "I say unto you," "son of David," and "from that time."

## No Ascension

Matthew began his Gospel by focusing the Jews upon the Lord Jesus as the Son of David, the rightful heir to the throne of David. He will close his Gospel in a figurative manner that beautifully climaxes this realization. Does he conclude, as Mark did, by recording the ascension of Christ back to heaven? No. You will find no ascension of Christ in Matthew.

What we do observe is Christ positioned on a mountain in Galilee imparting directions to His disciples. As mentioned earlier, mountains, in the figurative sense, symbolize kingdoms in the Bible. From a Jewish perspective, this scene is the climax of Matthew and completes the theme that he began in the very first verse. It is only made possible through the finished work at Calvary. Just before the curtain draws closed, we get a futuristic representation of Christ's kingdom established on earth. The subjects of the kingdom are before Him and resolutely worshipping their King (Matt. 28:17). God will keep His promise to Abraham, to David, to the Jewish people and to all those who heed the Gospel message and enter by faith into the kingdom of heaven.

# The Gospel of Mark

# "Behold My Servant"

*Behold My Servant, whom I uphold; mine elect, in whom My soul delighteth; I have put My spirit upon Him: He shall bring forth judgment to the Gentiles (Isa. 42:1).*

# A Serving Saviour

Throughout the Bible, God refers to a select few individuals as His servants. God applied the explicit title *"The Servant of the Lord"* to only two individuals in the Bible, Moses and Joshua. It is noted that this title is predominantly applied after their deaths; despite their faults, they were remembered by the Lord for finishing well. The less formal expression *"my servant"* is assigned by God to only ten individuals: Abraham, Job, Moses, Caleb, David, Isaiah, Eliakim, Israel, Zerubbabel, and the Lord Jesus.

One day when Satan had to present himself before God's throne in heaven, the Lord said to him, *"Have you considered **My servant Job**, that there is none like him on the earth, a blameless and upright man, one who fears God and shuns evil?" (Job 1:8, NKJV)*. God furnished a vivid character sketch of Job, whom He considered His servant. The proclamation brought an immediate challenge from Satan who, as we know, was allowed by God to initiate a series of horrendous circumstances to test Job's wherewithal. Satan, as a defeated foe, hates everything about the Lord Jesus. The last thing he wants now is people on earth who remind him of Christ and who are doing the will of God. These would be known in the Church Age as *"the servants of the Lord."* Consider Paul's exhortation to Timothy:

*Flee also youthful lusts; but pursue righteousness, faith, love, peace with those who call on the Lord out of a pure heart. But avoid foolish and ignorant disputes, knowing that they generate strife. And **a servant of the Lord** must not quarrel but be gentle to all, able to teach, patient... (2 Tim. 2:22-25, NKJV).*

As we ponder the Lord Jesus as God's servant, it must be emphasized that the revealed character of the servant of God is as important as what that servant does. The servant of the Lord represents God in character and conduct. Mark will show us the gentle, kind, humble nature of the Lord Jesus while enduring distress, rejection and hardship in His God-given ministry. So, when the Father proclaims to all *"Behold My Servant,"* it is an invitation to admire the Person as much as His tenacious ministry. It also, as with Job, invites the accusations and challenges of the wicked, which Christ endured without ever neglecting His lowly service to humanity. God's Servant willingly and selflessly spends and is spent for others and will be attacked and rejected for doing so. From this vantage point, Mark attests to man's superficial claim on Christ, not Christ's rightful claim on men.

## The Author

There is little doubt that John Mark wrote the Gospel of Mark. Church tradition is varied as to how much Peter influenced Mark's writing, but it seems plausible Peter would have conversed with Mark about the life of the Lord Jesus while they were working together in Babylon (1 Pet. 5:13) and perhaps later in Rome. It is quite possible that Peter was the divine instrument used in John Mark's conversion.

In the New Testament, our author is referred to by his compound Jewish/Gentile name, John Mark, three times and by his Latin name, Mark (Marcus), ten times; the latter became his common name. His mother Mary lived in Jerusalem and used their home as a gathering place for Christian meetings. We first meet Mark in Jerusalem in Acts 12; a prayer meeting was in his home (Acts 12:12). Paul and Barnabas had journeyed to Jerusalem to deliver a gift to the suffering saints from the Christians in Antioch. After completing this task, they returned to Antioch with John Mark (Acts 12:25), who was Barnabas' nephew (Col. 4:10). He would later sail with Paul and Barnabas on the first missionary journey to Crete and then Asia Minor. But shortly after arriving at Pamphylia, which was their third stop, John Mark abandoned Paul and Barnabas: *"Now when Paul and his company loosed from Paphos, they came to Perga in Pamphylia: and John departing from them returned to Jerusalem" (Acts 13:13).*

Paul and Barnabas finished their first missionary trip by returning to Antioch, their commending assembly. After wintering in Antioch, they agreed to again return to Asia, but a strong disagreement occurred between them concerning whether John Mark should be in their company: *"But Paul thought it not good to take him with them, who departed from them from Pamphylia, and went not with them to the work" (Acts 15:38).* John Mark had recovered from his lapse of faith and did indeed travel with Barnabas; Paul took Silas, and two missionary teams went out instead of one. Years later, just before being martyred for Christ, Paul acknowledged that Mark was a profitable servant in the ministry (2 Tim. 4:11).

Proverbs 24:16 reads, *"For a just man falleth seven times, and riseth up again; but the wicked shall fall into mischief."* In service to God, it is not falling that makes one a failure, but staying down, or should I say, wallowing in self-pity and nursing wounded pride. Falling is never an end in itself unless the servant of God determines it so. God wants us to succeed and bring Him glory by living for Christ. So, when you fall, learn from your mistake, rise up in the wisdom and strength of God, and walk by faith. Matthew, a Jewish official, wrote of the regal glory of the Lord Jesus. Who better to write of His humble service as the Servant of Jehovah than John Mark, a servant who had suffered total humiliation yet was still profitable to God?

## Content and Theme

Approximately ninety percent of Mark has parallel content in Matthew and Luke, yet the flavoring of these commonalities is different and more chronologically presented. Mark is the most brief and condensed of the Gospel accounts; very few key words or phrases are used repetitiously to accentuate certain points or to provide an outline of his work. In Matthew and Luke, angelic messengers and prophetic pronouncements through human agents introduced the Saviour, but not in Mark. His introduction is quite concise: a few verses to describe the ministry of John the Baptist and the Lord's baptism and temptation, but by verse fourteen of the first chapter, the Lord is preaching the kingdom Gospel message and pouring Himself out to humanity. The fact that Mark so abruptly brings us to the beginning of Christ's ministry fits well with his theme – Christ the humble and industrious servant of God.

Though brief in introduction, Mark safeguards against having a degraded view of God's Servant in his opening verse: *"The beginning of the Gospel of Jesus Christ, **the Son of God."*** Humanly speaking, it is natural to adopt a smug attitude about someone serving you, but Mark ensures that his readers understand that this was willful condescension by the Son of God. For this reason, the Lord never speaks of "My Father" or "Our Father" in Mark's record; His humble service to man, not His relationship with the Father, is paramount. But to ensure no confusion on the matter, Mark immediately guards against undermining the deity of Christ.

Mark contains few parables, four to be exact, whereas Matthew contains many more. Mark focuses more on the busy life of Christ in doing miracles and ministering to the broken hearted and the down and outers. Though few in number, one parable is peculiar to Mark, thus, prompting the question "Why?" Andrew Jukes answers this question:

> But as to that parable which is only here [in Mark], of "the Seed which grew secretly, first the blade, then the ear, and then the full corn," what is it but an encouragement to servants to sow in faith, and then leave results to Him who only can give increase?
>
> It seems to me as if the Lord Himself here spoke out of the abundance of His heart; that He was expressing His own assurance of a full return for all His sore travail; and that in prospect of His death He rejoiced in the thought that whether the sower "sleep or rise," the seed would yet spring up and increase greatly.[1]

Mark depicts Christ ministering to God's chosen people, while Matthew reveals Christ as testing Israel. Mark is addressed to a wider audience, the Romans, while Matthew is distinctly Jewish. At the time that Christ walked upon the earth, the Roman Empire was about 120 million people strong, and half of these were slaves. Unfortunately, slavery was the reality of that day; therefore, his Roman audience would readily understand and relate to the flavor of his writing.

Because Mark presents Christ as a lowly servant, almost no authoritative decrees by the Lord are presented; that would be out of place in Mark. No sentence is passed on Israel. No "woe" message to Pharisees or stinging "woe unto you" decrees are issued by Christ in Mark; these well mark Matthew. There is no Christ weeping over Jerusalem, as in Matthew. The Lord Jesus cleansed the temple twice during His three plus years of public service, once at the beginning and once at the end of His ministry. Concerning the first event, Mark merely records that the Lord entered into the temple, but nothing is said of His driving out the moneychangers or turning over their tables. In Mark, Jesus is serving man not pronouncing judgment upon him.

## The Way of the Lord

*"The voice of one crying in the wilderness,* **Prepare ye the way of the Lord***, make His paths straight" (Mark 1:3).* The Gospel of John is packed with **sevens**, a number speaking of perfection and completeness. It is used in John to declare the perfections of Christ's work and person. However, the Holy Spirit saw fit to include a sevenfold witness in the first thirteen verses of Mark's Gospel for the same purpose. Before beginning His lowly service to humanity in verse 14, *"the way of the Lord"* was well prepared. Mark ensured that his audience knew that the One who was in the form of a Servant was none other than God Himself. Hamilton Smith summarizes the seven testimonies of the divine glory of Christ:

v. 1    The first witness is the writer of the Gospel – Mark, by reminding us that He is *"Jesus Christ, the Son of God."*

vv. 2-3   Secondly, the prophets are quoted, as being witness of the glory of His Person.

vv. 4-8   Thirdly, we have the witness of John, the Forerunner, to the glory of the perfect Servant.

vv. 9-11    Fourthly, we have the witness of the voice from Heaven to the glory of Christ.

vv. 12-13   Fifthly, we have a brief allusion to the temptation in the wilderness. The temptation of our Lord in a wilderness became a witness to His infinite perfection whereby He overcame Satan.

v. 13       Sixthly, creation, itself, bears witness to the glory of His Person, for we read, He was *"with the wild beasts."* However much the beasts may fear men, they have no fear of this blessed Man, for He, indeed, is their Creator.

V. 13       Lastly, we read, *"the Angels ministered unto Him."* The One who came to be the Servant is, Himself, served by angelic hosts. He is none less than *"the Son," "the First Begotten,"* of Whom, when He comes into the world, it is said, *"Let all the angels of God worship Him."*[2]

## Designed Omissions

Perhaps the first obvious omission is that Mark includes no genealogies. In fact, no mention is made of Christ's birth or childhood. This omission is in keeping with the perspective of Christ's serving ministry. In Mark, it would not be genealogies or childhood history, but what the Lord did for others that established His credentials as the servant of Jehovah.

Because the Lord Jesus is presented as ministering to instead of commanding others, no mention is made in Mark of the Sermon on the Mount. No Kingdom Manifesto is proclaimed. Consequently, authoritative expressions are seldom found in Mark, as compared to the other Gospel accounts. Divine or exalted titles pertaining to the Lord Jesus are also rare in Mark. He is not called Emmanuel – "God with us." Of the twenty-eight times Jesus is referred to as "the Son of God" in the four Gospels, only three are found in Mark. In Mark, the Lord is referred to by the reverent title, "Christ," only twice. Matthew refers to Jesus as Christ four times in the first chapter alone. The Lord Jesus is referred to as the "son of David" only once in Mark; Matthew applies the title ten times. Also, no enlisting of Jesus as king is found in Mark. Mark is the only writer to refer to the Lord as *"the son of Mary" (Mark 6:3).* The Lord was born into His mother's low social status ensuring He was acquainted with a simplistic and austere way of life. The Lord Jesus, as God's Servant, knew first-hand about hard work and redeeming time.

## Repent and Believe

One of the most beautiful panoramic views of the differing vantage points of Christ is seen in the Gospel message itself. Each writer declares the "good news" message but does so in a way that best resembles his associated "behold view" of the living Message. Thus, each writer emphasizes different aspects of the kingdom Gospel message.

### Matthew
*From that time Jesus began to preach, and to say, **Repent:** for the kingdom of heaven is at hand (Matt. 4:17).*

### Mark
*Now after that John was put in prison, Jesus came into Galilee, preaching the Gospel of the kingdom of God. And saying, The time is fulfilled, and the kingdom of God is at hand: **repent ye, and believe** the Gospel (Mark 1:14-15).*

## Luke

*The Spirit of the Lord is upon Me, because He hath anointed Me to **preach the Gospel to the poor**; He hath sent Me to heal the brokenhearted, **to preach deliverance** to the captives, and recovering of sight to the blind, **to set at liberty** them that are bruised, to preach **the acceptable year of the Lord** (Luke 4:18-19).*

*I tell you, Nay: but, **except ye repent**, ye shall all likewise **perish** (Luke 13:5).*

## John

*But as many as received Him, to them gave He power to become the sons of God, even to them that **believe on His name**. Which **were born**, not of blood, nor of the will of the flesh, nor of the will of man, but **of God** (John 1:12-13).*

*Jesus answered and said unto him, Verily, verily, I say unto thee, Except a man **be born again**, he cannot see the kingdom of God (John 3:3).*

*He that **believeth** on the Son hath **everlasting life**: and he that **believeth not** the Son shall not see life; but the **wrath of God** abideth on him (John 3:36).*

There is but one Gospel message, yet each writer highlights varying aspects of the Gospel as it directly relates to his associated theme. This variance is really one of the most astoundingly contrasting facets of the Gospel accounts. It is noted that, though Mark is the shortest Gospel, he refers to the word "Gospel" more than the other writers do; John does not even mention the term. Matthew's authority theme stresses "repentance" eleven times, but only three times does he speak of the necessity to believe in the Lord Jesus. In fact, in Matthew, the Lord spends more time criticizing the Jews for not believing John's message of repentance than for not believing upon Him.

Mark stresses the need to both repent and to believe in Christ to be saved, but there is clearly a heavier focus on believing. He directly speaks of believing in Christ nearly a dozen times and of the necessity to repent only four times. Since the Lord is not lauding His kingly authority in Mark, repentance is of a secondary emphasis. It would, however, require real faith to believe upon a lowly Servant for salvation.

Luke speaks of believing in the Lord five times but addresses the matter of repentance fourteen times. The beloved physician instead employs terms in his Gospel which appeal to human need and suffering, such as "perishing" (Luke 13:3, 5). "Perishing" speaks of dying, and Luke speaks of it more often than the other Gospel writers. With all sincerity, Luke is asking his audience, "Would you like to be saved from dying?" On behalf of Christ, he petitions the sick, the suffering, and the brokenhearted; all those suffering under the effects of sin. "Would you desire to be relieved of your distresses and infirmities?" These aspects are contained within the framework of Luke's Gospel presentation. The Lord feels our infirmities, the painful consequences of our sin. He desires to save the sinner from eternal judgment and also to relieve the agonizing aftermath of sin.

The exalted tone of John's Gospel expresses the heavenly perspective of the Gospel message. Matthew and Luke stress repentance, for one must acknowledge their sins before salvation can be obtained, but John simply and precisely declares the overall spiritual situation: In God is life, and apart from God is death. Speaking of Christ, John writes: *"All things were made by Him; and without Him was not any thing made that was made. In Him was life; and the life was the light of men" (John 1:3-4).* John stresses the plain truth of the matter –

man is spiritually dead in the world and must be born again (John 3:3) and made alive (John 5:21). How is this accomplished? By believing. *"For God so loved the world, that He gave His only begotten Son, that whosoever believeth in Him should not perish, but have everlasting life" (John 3:16).* Consequently, the words "repent" and "forgive" are not found in John's account, but the matter of believing is emphasized ninety-nine times! John's message could be summarized as: "Man is dead in the world. Eternal life is only in Christ. Do you believe this?"

Perhaps the following improvised story will help us understand how each writer relates to the Gospel message preached by Christ. Imagine a man fishing on a large flat rock adjoining a fast-flowing river. He is a stranger to the area, but while driving along the river, he spotted what he thought would be a great fishing hole. He couldn't resist the temptation, so he quickly pulled over and grabbed his fly rod and tackle box. His first cast lands a sizable brown trout, and while leaning over to pull it from the water, he slips off the rock he has been standing upon and falls into the frigid water. The situation is desperate because the man does not know how to swim and the cold deep water is quickly numbing his muscles. Fortunately for him, a huge log is floating down the river near him, and with a few desperate lunges, he is able to grasp it. Although he is debilitated from his near drowning experience, he musters up his remaining strength to cling to the tree. Though chilled to the bone, he begins to calm down and breathe a bit easier; he feels safe and is confident that he will eventually float near the shore.

His moment of composure is interrupted by cries from behind him. He glances over his shoulder to see five individuals running along the shoreline; one has a long rope in his hand. As they draw nearer, he is able to discern their warning – "huge waterfall ahead" – "certain death!" The man, not being familiar with the river, has no idea whether this information is true. Since he cannot see the approaching doom, he remains determined to grip his only means of safety, the log. One individual on the shore, named Matthew, yells out "This man with the rope is the park ranger. He can save you from going over the waterfall, but you must let go of the log." Another man, named Mark, cries out, "Yes, when this man throws you the rope, you must let go of the log to grasp the rope; he will then pull you to safety for he is strong and able."

The third man, Luke, shouts, "You will perish if you don't let go of the log and grab hold of the rope. This man with the rope knows how cold and afraid you are, and he can help you." Finally, the fourth man, John, declares, "Your situation is desperate. You are going to die. You must grasp the rope and trust this man with your life – he has saved everyone who has ever trusted him."

Repentance is stressed in the letting go of the log, which might be named "Infant Baptism," or "Good Deeds," or "Church Attendance." Believing is demonstrated by the grasping of the rope that is anchored to a secure object. Repentance literally means "to turn," and demonstrates an understanding of our desperate situation; we are sinners and could plummet into hell at any moment. We are merely one heartbeat away from eternity. Repentance is agreeing with God about our spiritual condition and that He is right about this matter of sin. *"For godly sorrow worketh repentance to salvation not to be repented of: but the sorrow of the world worketh death" (2 Cor. 7:10).*

Repentance loosens its grip on self-pride, self-works and human traditions and chooses to grip the *"the truth and the life,"* the Lord Jesus. Repentance and faith are different but very much connected. If the man only let go of the log, he would still perish, either by drowning or over the falls. To be saved, one must let go of the log then grip the rope. One cannot grip the log and the rope simultaneously; that individual would still go over the falls. *"For by grace are ye saved through faith; and that not of yourselves: it is the gift of God: Not of works, lest any man should boast" (Eph. 2:8-9).* To be saved, the man had to reckon his condition as desperate, understand he had only one means to safety, then act upon that means which required letting go of the log and grasping the rope. Salvation is obtained only by grace through faith, but repentance must precede an exercise of faith. Because the reality of having no other escape from certain death is understood – true saving faith has a continuing reality. Though doubts may creep in from time to time, true faith abides for it reckons the seriousness of the situation to be real. Genuine faith holds on to the rope which is eternally secure in Christ.

Each evangelist is proclaiming the good news of Jesus Christ but from different perspectives. It is all the truth, related and all one message, but it is uniquely presented for the purpose of seeing the fullness of Christ.

## Specific Presentations of Christ

The manner in which the Lord spoke of Himself or in which the disciples addressed Him is generally consistent with the theme of each Gospel writer. Note the differences in the following examples; each is a parallel account of the same event.

### At the Transfiguration
*Verily I say unto you, there be some standing here, which shall not taste of death, till they see the Son of man coming in His kingdom (Matt. 16:28).*

*And He said unto them, verily I say unto you, that there be some of them that stand here, which shall not taste of death,* *till they have **seen the kingdom of God** come with power (Mark 9:1).*

Matthew stresses Christ coming into His kingdom, while Mark simply notes that the kingdom will come.

### Triumphal Entry of Christ (Jerusalem)

*And the multitudes that went before, and that followed, cried, saying, Hosanna to **the Son of David**: Blessed is He that cometh in the name of the Lord; Hosanna in the highest (Matt. 21:9).*

*And they that went before, and they that followed, cried, saying, Hosanna; Blessed is **He** that cometh in the name of the Lord (Mark 11:9).*

Matthew stresses that the one coming in the name of the Lord is the Son of David, while Mark applies a simple pronoun, "He."

### How the Disciples Addressed Christ:

#### In a Boat During a Storm

*And His disciples came to Him, and awoke Him, saying, **Lord,** save us: we perish (Matt. 8:25).*

*And He was in the hinder part of the ship, asleep on a pillow: and they awake Him, and say unto Him, **Master,** carest thou not that we perish? (Mark 4:38).*

### Just Prior to the Transfiguration

*From that time forth began Jesus to shew unto His disciples, how that he must go unto Jerusalem, and suffer many things of the elders and chief priests and scribes, and be killed, and be raised again the third day. Then Peter took Him, and began to rebuke **Him**, saying, Be it far from thee, **Lord**: this shall not be unto thee (Matt. 16:21-22).*

*And He spake that saying openly. And Peter took Him, and began to rebuke **Him** (Mark 8:32).*

### At the Last Supper

*And they were exceeding sorrowful, and began every one of them to say unto Him, **Lord**, is it I? (Matt. 26:22).*

*And they began to be sorrowful, and to say unto Him one by one, Is it I? And another said, Is it I? (Mark 14:19).*

Matthew ascribes titles of prominence to the Lord Jesus and acknowledges His kingly authority, while Mark speaks of Christ from a humble perspective often applying lesser titles than Matthew, such as Teacher and Master, or non-descriptive pronouns. Luke frequently refers to the Lord as the Son of Man, while John, more than any other writer, assigns the title *"the Son of God"* to the Lord Jesus. Although the disciples never referred to the Lord simply as "Jesus" after they understood who He was, the different Gospel writers used expressions and titles fitting their "behold" theme of Christ.

# A Busy Servant

Twelve of Mark's sixteen chapters begin with the word "and," and the far majority of the verses in Mark begin with conjunctions and adverbs such as "and," "now," and "then." For example, Mark 1 contains 45 verses, and 35 of them begin with *"And...."* More specifically, many verses in Mark begin *"And Jesus..."* or *"And He...."* Mark is careful to present a serving Saviour to his audience: "And Jesus was doing this, and Jesus was doing that."

But he doesn't stop there. In order for the reader to gain a higher sense of the Lord's exhausting ministry, he adds further description to the verbs describing the Lord's service, employing words such as "forthwith," and "immediately." This is accomplished by repeatedly applying two Greek adverbs: *eutheos* meaning "directly," and *euthus* meaning "at once." How are these adverbs applied in the other Gospels? Here is the breakdown. Keep in mind that Mark has only sixteen chapters compared to Matthew's twenty-eight.

| Adverb | Matthew | Mark | Luke | John |
|---|---|---|---|---|
| *Eutheos* | *15* | *40* | *8* | *4* |
| *Euthus* | *4* | *6* | *2* | *3* |
| **Total** | **19** | **46** | **10** | **7** |

The frequency of usage in Mark is unmistakably distinctive! Those of the Lord's servants who are involved in various "full-time" ministries understand, in a measure, non-stop ministry exhaustion (Many elders and other saints know this all too well also.). Can you imagine the life of the Lord Jesus? Day in and day out, at any time of day or night, people were coming to him with their problems and ailments. Those rejecting His message confronted Him continuously. No wonder He fell asleep in the stern of a boat and didn't wake up when the boat was being tossed to and fro in a violent storm. Add to this His fervent prayer life. Even though His life was marked by a constant state of physical exhaustion, He still arose early, often while it was yet dark, to spend time conversing with His Father. Mark presents to us not just a serving Saviour, but One that incessantly, steadily and promptly served others. The Lord Jesus poured His life out to satisfy the needs of others.

## Hands and Eyes

Mark often refers to the Lord as looking at and touching others. In so doing, Mark presents a Servant that is cognizant of the needs of others – the Lord didn't have tunnel vision to the cross but wide-scoping discernment of others around Him. Each passing day brought the Saviour even nearer to Calvary, but along the way, He lived each day to serve others. The Lord recognized essential needs, then personally advanced to help.

Mark speaks of the Lord looking upon or beholding others nine different times; the other Gospels often omit the "looking" aspect of the event. The following examples illustrate this Gospel's distinction of "looking":

### Rebuke of Peter
*Then Peter took Him, and began to rebuke Him, saying, Be it far from thee, Lord: this shall not be unto Thee. But He turned, and said unto Peter, Get thee behind Me, Satan...* (Matt. 16:22-23).

*And He spake that saying openly. And Peter took Him, and began to rebuke Him. But when He had turned about and* **looked on His disciples**, *He rebuked Peter, saying, Get thee behind Me, Satan...* (Mark 8:32-33).

### Dialogue with the Rich Young Ruler
*Then Jesus* **beholding him** *loved him, and said unto him, One thing thou lackest: go thy way, sell whatsoever thou hast, and give to the poor, and thou shalt have treasure in heaven: and come, take up the cross, and follow Me* (Mark 10:21).

*Now when Jesus heard these things, He said unto him, Yet lackest thou one thing: sell all that thou hast, and distribute unto the poor, and thou shalt have treasure in heaven: and come, follow Me (Luke 18:22).*

## Entering the Temple after Triumphal Entry (Jerusalem)
*And Jesus went into the temple of God, and cast out all them that sold and bought in the temple, and overthrew the tables of the moneychangers, and the seats of them that sold doves (Matt. 21:12).*

*And Jesus entered into Jerusalem, and into the temple: and when **He had looked round** about upon all things... (Mark 11:11).*

For a servant to be effective, he must be able to discern the true needs of others, then perform the service to them that will be most beneficial. As the Lord demonstrates in His ministry, this service may include help, encouragement, exhortation, or even rebuke. Thus, Mark shows us the discerning nature of Christ's ministry by mentioning the Lord's looking at and beholding others. But Mark doesn't stop with mere information of need; he also speaks of the Lord's hands touching the distressed. As the following examples show, this point is often excluded from the parallel accounts in the other Gospels.

## Healing of Simon Peter's Mother-in-Law
*But Simon's wife's mother lay sick of a fever, and anon they tell Him of her. And **He came and took her by the hand**, and lifted her up; and immediately the fever left her, and she ministered unto them (Mark 1:30-31).*

*And He arose out of the synagogue, and entered into Simon's house. And Simon's wife's mother was taken with a great fever; and they besought Him for her. And **He stood over*** *her, and rebuked the fever; and it left her: and immediately she arose and ministered unto them  (Luke 4:38-39).*

### Healing of the Deaf and Dumb Individual
*And they bring unto Him one that was deaf, and had an impediment in his speech; and they beseech Him to put His hand upon him. And He took him aside from the multitude, and **put His fingers into his ears**, and He spit, and touched his tongue... (Mark 7:32-33).*

No other Gospel records this specific miracle.

### Healing of the Demon Possessed Boy
*And Jesus rebuked the demon, and it came out of him; and the child was cured from that very hour (Matt. 17:18, NKJV).*

*But Jesus **took him by the hand**, and lifted him up; and he arose (Mark 9:27).*

In all, I find three references in Matthew, six in Mark, two in Luke and none in John of the Lord compassionately touching others to heal them. Apparently, to avoid using the term "touched," John states that Jesus anointed the eyes of the man born blind to heal him (John 9:6). Of the thirty-seven occurrences of the various forms of the word "touch" in the Gospels, only one reference is found in John, when the Lord insisted that Mary not **hold** Him (This was after He had appeared to her on resurrection day.).

Mark demonstrates to his audience that the Servant of the Lord wonderfully discerns the needs of others, then quickly works with His hands to assist them: *"Behold My Servant."*

# How Did Christ Serve?

George MacDonald once said, "God never gave a man a thing to do concerning which it were irreverent to ponder how the Son of God would have done it."[3] In depicting the Servant of Jehovah, Mark provides the perfect character sketch of a true godly servant. The Lord Jesus teaches us through His selfless example what true servanthood is all about. Just prior to his death, Paul's final exhortation to his spiritual son Timothy was to fulfill his ministry: *"Preach the word; be instant **in season, out of season**; reprove, rebuke, exhort with all longsuffering and doctrine" (2 Tim. 4:2).* Mark shows a Christ who knew all about "in season," and "out of season" ministry, He was on duty at all times! How might the Lord's service to others be described? Mark provides a complete character sketch.

**The Lord's service was motivated by love.** *"And Jesus moved with compassion..." (Mark 1:41).* The Lord teaches us that the only true motive for Christian service to God is love and, nonetheless, that the only reason to serve others is love. Biblical love initiates sacrificial giving! *"**For God so loved** the world that **He gave** His only begotten Son..."* Mark notes the Lord's self-sacrificing example throughout his Gospel (Mark 3:20; 4:35-36; 4:38; 6:31; 7:34; and 8:12). Love is discerning and understands what is best for the individual one seeks to serve. Love, not pity, must be our reason to serve those in need, or we may unknowingly provide for others to sin or interfere with the chastening hand of God in their lives.

**The Lord served others before Himself.**

*And the multitude cometh together again, so that **they could not so much as eat bread** (Mark 3:20).*

*And He said to them, "Come aside by yourselves to a deserted place and rest a while." **For there were many coming and going, and they did not even have time to eat.** So they departed to a deserted place in the boat by themselves. **But the multitudes saw them departing, and many knew Him and ran there on foot from all the cities. They arrived before them and came together to Him** (Mark 6:31-33, NKJV).*

The Lord was so busy serving others, so disposed to mankind, so available to the distressed, that He often had no time to properly care for Himself. On another occasion, we find the Lord asleep in the stern of a boat, during daylight hours and while in the midst of a raging storm – physical exhaustion and emotional fatigue frequented His body, yet we never read of Him complaining once.

**The Lord served with tenacity.** Practically everyone with a problem, and at least a bit of faith, were petitioning the Lord for help.

*And He healed many that were sick of divers diseases, and cast out many devils; and suffered not the devils to speak, because they knew Him (Mark 1:34).*

*For He had healed many; insomuch that they pressed upon Him for to touch Him, as many as had plagues (Mark 3:10).*

The disciples said to the Lord, *"All men seek for Thee" (Mark 1:37).* This statement highlights the immensity of Christ's counseling and healing ministry. Wouldn't you want to go to a physician who had a one-hundred percent success rate of curing patients and mending families?

**The Lord did not seek popularity.** What was the Lord's response when His disciples informed Him that *"all men seek for Thee?"* The Lord replied, *"Let us go into the next towns" (Mark 1:38).* He could have used the opportunity to promote Himself and gain a fan club, but He was more interested in the quality of His disciples than quantity of the followers. Arthur Pink writes:

> We like to boast of the crowds that attend our ministry. But the perfect Servant of God never courted popularity, He shunned it! And when His disciples came and told Him – no doubt with pleasurable pride *"All men seek for Thee,"* His immediate response was, *"Let us go!".*[4]

Mark clearly furnishes a progressive attitude of humility by the Lord in response to his instant fame. At first, He tolerated the popularity, then He shunned it, and finally He avoided it altogether:

> *And **immediately His fame spread abroad** throughout all the region round about Galilee (Mark 1:28).*

> *But **Jesus withdrew himself** with his disciples to the sea: and a great multitude from Galilee followed him, and from Judaea (Mark 3:7).*

> *And straightway his ears were opened, and the string of his tongue was loosed, and he spake plain. And **He charged them that they should tell no man**: but the more he charged them, so much the more a great deal they published it (Mark 7:35-36).*

> *After that He put his hands again upon his eyes, and made him look up: and he was restored, and saw every man clearly. And*

*He sent him away to his house, saying,* **Neither go into the town, nor tell it to any in the town** *(Mark 8:25-26).*

*And they departed thence, and passed through Galilee; and* **He would not that any man should know it** *(Mark 9:30).*

It is evident from Mark's various healing accounts that the Lord did not desire fame or popularity but rather that He desired to demonstrate that genuine service for others is veiled in secrecy. May each of us learn of Christ and pursue His meek and lowly example.

**The Lord served compassionately**. He had His eyes open to the needs of others; He was discerning – *"He looked upon them."* What do a leper, four blind men, and three disciples have in common? They were all touched by Christ to satisfy a need. The leper was a social outcast and longed to be embraced. For the blind, every clumsy step ventured into the unknown, but the Lord lifted this darkness and gave their souls security. At His transfiguration, the fearful disciples were comforted in a time of panic: *"And Jesus came and touched them, and said, Arise, and be not afraid. And when they had lifted up their eyes, they saw no man, save Jesus only" (Matt. 17:7-8).* Why didn't the Lord just speak a good word to these individuals? He understood that a loving touch could convey what words couldn't. Let us not fear to reach out and touch those in need, so they, too, might see *"no man save Jesus!"*

The Lord cared about the possessed, the sick, the blind, the deaf, the mute, the paralyzed, the diseased, the suffering, and the dead. He often touched those He healed (Mark 1:30-31). There is a whole world of needy people, and Christ teaches us to open our eyes to see them and not to be afraid to share some skin with those in need. Listening and touching are important gestures of love.

**The Lord continued serving despite constant opposition.** Before the events of Calvary, nearly twenty references of the Lord doing ministry in the face of challenges, disdain, and rejection are found in Mark (2:6-7; 2:16; 2:24; 3:2; 3:6; 3:22; 5:17; 5:40; 6:3; 6:5; 7:1-2; 8:11; 10:2; 11:27-28; 12:13; 12:18; 12:28; 14:4, …). Christ shows us that if you are doing anything for the Lord, you will be criticized and suffer for it, so expect it. The same pharisaical attitude that existed during Christ's first advent still continues unto this day. The Lord Jesus left us a self-sacrificing example to follow. A true servant cares nothing for himself, about what he is asked to do, or about what others think of him; the only focus must be to do the Master's bidding.

> *For this is thankworthy, if a man for conscience toward God endure grief, suffering wrongfully. For what glory is it, if, when ye be buffeted for your faults, ye shall take it patiently? but if, when ye do well, and suffer for it, ye take it patiently, this is acceptable with God. For even hereunto were ye called: because Christ also suffered for us, leaving us an example, that ye should follow his steps (1 Pet. 2:19-21).*

**The Lord was a good administrator.** The Lord redeemed the most out of His time on earth and showed good managerial skills while serving. Concerning evangelism, the Lord sent His disciples *"forth two by two" (Mark 6:7, NKJV).* In accomplishing the miracle of feeding the 5000 (plus women and children), the Lord had the people sit down in ranks of hundreds and fifties (Mark 6:39-40). In application, might we, before taking on new ministries and responsibilities, learn discipline, good organizational skills, and efficient and frugal means of accomplishing God-directed ministry. Why would the Lord give us more to do for the kingdom of God, if we have not learned to be efficient in accomplishing what He has already requested of us? Many of the Lord's people today cannot respond with their time or finances to the urgent needs of the mission field because they are strapped with debt and, thus, enslaved to an employer or business. May we all learn from the Lord's example of managing every task well.

**The Lord prayed before serving.** *"And in the morning, rising up a great while before day, He went out, and departed into a solitary place, and there prayed" (Mark 1:35). "And when He had sent them away, He departed into a mountain to pray" (Mark 6:46).* Matthew records Christ praying on only three separate occasions, but Mark and Luke often refer to the Lord's prayer life. This difference is in keeping with the Gospel themes, as the exalted King would be less dependent upon help from above than the lowly human Servant.

How often do we surge ahead of the perfect plan of God? Waiting is often harder than working, for we feel compelled to do something, but often it is not to pray. Prayer demonstrates complete faith in the Lord to initiate, direct, and complete each matter of our lives according to His will (1 Jn. 5:14). Besides moving the hand of God to affect His glory, prayer transforms our hearts by conforming our thinking to the mind of Christ.

Hudson Taylor, who labored for the kingdom in China, had three important principles concerning prayer:

1. You can work without praying, but it is a bad plan.
2. You cannot pray in earnest without working.
3. Do not be so busy with work for Christ that you have no strength left for praying. True praying requires strength.[5]

Warren Wiersbe writes, "Prayer is not an escape from responsibility; it is our *response* to God's *ability*. True prayer energizes us for service and battle."[6]

Before choosing His disciples, the Lord spent an entire night in prayer (Luke 6:12). The Lord prayed before feeding the 5000, just prior to Peter's pronouncement that He was *"the Christ the Son of the living God,"* and before raising Lazarus from the dead. The Lord's final hours before Calvary were spent in prayer. The prayer life of the Lord Jesus was so intense and so fruitful that on one occasion the disciples asked the Saviour to teach them how to pray. They wanted in on the blessings of prayer. How about you? How is your prayer life? We should follow the Lord's example – prayer preceded service and followed accomplishments – prayer preceded crisis and followed achievements. *"And He spake a parable unto them to this end, **that men ought always to pray, and not to faint"** (Luke 18:1).*

## Key Words and Phrases

Mark's brevity presents his audience with fewer key words and phrases than the other Gospel writers. Yet, as previously identified, there are some words and phrases, which clearly sustain his overall servant theme of the Saviour. These are: "forthwith," "immediately," "shortly," "straightway, " "touch," "looked," and "and."

## The Great Commission

The closing verses of Mark's Gospel record the final words of the Lord Jesus to His disciples before ascending back to Heaven, which is commonly referred to as the Great Commission. What is striking is that even in the commissioning of His disciples, which was after Calvary, after the grave, and after Christ's resurrection, Mark still maintains the servant vantage point of the Saviour. Compare Matthew's and Mark's commissioning records:

> And Jesus came and spoke to them, saying, **"All authority has been given to Me in heaven and on earth... teaching them to observe all things that I have commanded you...."** (Matt. 28:18-20, NKJV).

> And He said to them, "Go into all the world and preach the Gospel to every creature. He who believes and is baptized will be saved; but **he who does not believe will be condemned.** And **these signs** will follow those who believe...." (Mark 16:15-18, NKJV).

Matthew's account clearly shows Christ as the Lord of the kingdom, whereas Mark omits the authority and commanding aspects of the commission and, instead, highlights the lowly path of God's servant, which includes the possibility of rejection and the pouring out of oneself to meet the needs of others.

In his book *Here's the Difference*, William MacDonald highlights another important distinction in the commissioning of the disciples as recorded in the four Gospels:

> At the end of each Gospel, the Lord Jesus commissioned His disciples, but notice the different emphasis each time:
> Matthew – make disciples, preaching and teaching (28:19)
> Mark – preach the Gospel (16:15)
> Luke – witness (24:48)
> John – follow me (21:19-22, spoken to Peter, but applies to all)[7]

## The Ascension and More

In just fourteen verses, Mark introduces the Lord Jesus as the Son of God and expedites Him into active ministry as the Servant of Jehovah. **And** Jesus steadily worked until they nailed

His worn out and beaten body to a cross. On resurrection day, the Lord issued, to His stunned disciples, the Great Commission decree just discussed. Mark then concludes His Gospel by upholding the central theme he has focused upon throughout:

> *So then after the Lord had spoken unto them, he was received up into heaven, and sat on the right hand of God. And they went forth, and preached everywhere, **the Lord working with them,** and confirming the word with signs following. Amen (Mark 16:19-20).*

Verse 19 records the ascension of the Lord Jesus back into heaven, thus, a splendid climax to conclude Mark's story. However, that was not what the Holy Spirit had in mind, for He inspired Mark to add one more verse. In doing so, every disciple since that day understands that Christ labors with them. In Matthew, Christ's authority in directing the disciples is prominent throughout: *"Jesus sent them forth." "He commanded them," "go not," and "but go."* Mark, however, alludes to an aspect of the Commission which Matthew does not: *"the Lord working with them."* We do not labor for the kingdom alone or in vain, for it is His work, and He labors with us to accomplish it – we are His eyes to discern the needs of others and His hands to serve them. Paul informed the believers at Corinth, *"we are laborers together with God" (1 Cor. 3:9).* Christ labored with His disciples after commissioning them, and He still labors with His saints today.

With earnest gratefulness and loving appreciation, God the Father proclaimed to the far reaches of creation itself, "Behold My Servant!" His meek and humble character, His compassion for the suffering, and His resolute spirit in the face of opposition invite us to follow His example and to be true "servants of God." True love needs no title to serve, just the power to do so.

# The Gospel of Luke

# "Behold The Man"

*And speak unto him, saying, Thus speaketh the Lord of hosts, saying, **Behold the Man** whose name is The Branch; and He shall grow up out of His place, and He shall build the temple of the Lord (Zech 6:12).*

# God was Manifest in Flesh

One night on a lonely hillside, some 2000 years ago, shepherds were dazzled by the sudden appearance of an angel, and then a whole host of angels praising God. The message was profound: *"Fear not: for, behold, I bring you good tidings of great joy, which shall be **to all people**. For unto you **is born** this day in the city of David **a Saviour, which is Christ the Lord"** (Luke 2:10-11).* Through a birth relationship, Jesus Christ became connected with all people as the Saviour. Man could not make Him a Saviour; He was born Saviour of the world. Through birth, Christ's humanity was established – a link *"to all people."* As a man, He would likewise experience all the pangs of living upon a cursed planet and, before dying, feel the very condemnations He, Himself, had imputed to humanity in the Garden of Eden. Luke skillfully captures the anguish of these aspects of the Lord's life.

Luke, as Andrew Jukes puts it, is the writer who "sees Christ as the Son of Adam or the Son of Man, not so much connected with a kingdom, or the Servant of God, [but] as the One whose sympathies as a Man linked Him with Adam's fallen and ruined children."[1]

William Kelly beautifully describes the theme of Luke's Gospel in one deep and rather long respire:

The Holy Ghost undertakes to show us Christ as the one who brought to light all the moral springs of the heart of man, and at the same time the perfect grace of God in dealing with man as he is; therein, too, the divine wisdom in Christ which made its way through the world, the lovely grace, too, which attracted man when utterly confounded and broken down enough to cast himself upon what God is.[2]

## The Author

*"The beloved physician,"* as Paul calls Luke, was Paul's companion on many missionary journeys. Luke handles detail meticulously. Besides his conversations with Paul and other apostles, his keen eye notes many details that are simply passed over in the other Gospels. He is the only Gentile writer in all of Scripture and the only one to write a Gospel sequel, the book of Acts. His authorship is soundly confirmed through the information and style of Acts.

## The Gentile Flavor

The Gospel of Luke was written by a Gentile and to a Gentile audience. Paul clearly distinguishes Luke from "those of the circumcision." Because Luke's Gospel has a non-Jewish Flavor, certain details and narratives in Luke are not mentioned in Matthew, Mark and John. Note the Gentile character in Luke's introduction and, nonetheless, his objective of delivering a full and accurate account of the life of the Lord Jesus Christ.

> *Forasmuch as many have taken in hand **to set forth in order a declaration** of those things which are most surely believed among us, even as they **delivered them unto us**, which from the beginning were eyewitnesses, and ministers of the word; **It seemed good to me also**, having had perfect understanding of **all things from the very first, to write unto thee in order,** most excellent **Theophilus**, That thou mightest know the*

*certainty of those things, wherein thou hast been instructed (Luke 1:1-4).*

Twice in the opening sentence, Luke announces that he is declaring, in an "orderly" means, what he knows to be truth from the testimonies of multiple eyewitnesses (He does not specifically refer to Matthew and Mark.). Luke's personal compulsion to proclaim what he knew to be true would then be guided, arranged and constrained by the Holy Spirit to present an "orderly" account of the humanity of Christ *"from the very first."* This focus is why Luke provides such an in-depth account of the conception and birth of Christ – his foundation of the humanity of Christ is like no other.

Orderly does not necessarily mean chronological, but it does mean that he has organized the pertinent historical, political, moral, and spiritual content in a way which best relates to the human aspects of Christ's life and teachings. Sometimes teachings and narratives will be grouped together to provide an orderly presentation of a spiritual theme or to highlight human emotions or motives rather than to maintain chronological completeness. For example, the genealogy of Christ in chapter 3 seems out of place. Matthew begins with pedigree to prove royal lineage, but Luke waits thirty years to note the genealogy of Christ. Why?

Christ entered into a season of prayer promptly after His baptism. At that time, the Holy Spirit descended upon Him in the form of a dove, and the Father Himself declared from heaven, *"Thou art My beloved Son; in Thee I am well pleased."* Luke then injects the lineage of Christ to show that, though He came from a "seed of the woman," He was a representative of Adam on earth. The genealogy ends with *"who was the son of Adam, who was the son of God."* Where the first Adam failed, the Second, rather the Last, Adam would not. Immediately after this divine proclamation, the evil tempter assaulted the Lord for forty days. The Last Adam, the Son of God, triumphed over Satan – His righteous and holy character had been thoroughly proven. Luke waits two chapters to introduce the genealogy of Christ so that He might introduce his audience to the Last Adam, who was not human in the same way we are, but was proven to be sinless and perfect. Jesus Christ was God's replacement representative for the first Adam (Rom. 5:12-21).

Not only is Luke the only Gentile writer in Scripture, but he also addresses both of his written works, Acts being the other, to his Greek friend Theophilus. Luke's personalized salutation acquaints us immediately with a strong appeal to "human affection" which will characterize his Gospel. Theophilus means "beloved of God," and Luke's salutation serves as a testimony that the Gentiles are beloved of God. Mark wrote to the Romans, but Luke is setting forth an appeal to the Greeks concerning Christ. The Greeks prided themselves on intellectual observations and sought to apply knowledge and improve themselves (1 Cor. 1:22). They would be very interested in Luke's presentation of the "perfect" man and in a writing style that was well ordered and full of detail.

Besides the introduction, mentioned above, the following portions of Luke's Gospel are distinctly Gentile in application:

Only Luke makes mention of the Gentile aspects of the ministries of Elijah and Elisha: *"Elijah sent except to Zarephath, in the **region of Sidon**, to a woman who was a widow. And many lepers were in Israel in the time of Elisha the prophet, and none of them was cleansed except **Naaman the Syrian"** (Luke 4:26-27, NKJV)*

The parable of **"The Good Samaritan"** is only found in Luke (Luke 10). It is the story of a Gentile who loved his needy neighbor. The hard-hearted religious Jews of the day had no compassion for the injured man, but those whom the Jews considered "dogs" showed love.

On one occasion, the Lord healed ten lepers (nine Jews, and **one Samaritan**). The nine Jews thought their religion (the temple) was more important than thanking the One who had healed them. Not so for the Samaritan, he alone turned back to *"give glory to God."* Christ asked, *"Were there not ten cleansed? But where are the nine? There are not found that returned to give glory to God, save this stranger.... Arise, go thy way; thy faith hath made thee whole"* (Luke 17:17-19). Ten lepers were cleansed, but only one Gentile was saved that day.

On the Tuesday before He was crucified, the Lord Jesus led his disciples up the Mount of Olives to provide final instructions and to preview the details of the forthcoming Tribulation Period with them. During this discourse, the Lord declared that *"Jerusalem shall be trodden down **of the Gentiles**, until the times of the Gentiles be fulfilled"* (Luke 21:24). The other Gospels do not record this detail, though many of the prophets in the Old Testament, such as Ezekiel, Joel and Zechariah, do.

During the same dissertation, the Lord also mentioned, *"Behold the fig tree, **and all the trees**"* (Luke 21:29). Matthew only mentions the fig tree, which, in my opinion, represents religious Israel (Jer. 24) and is distinct from political Israel (represented by a vine – Isa. 5:2; Luke 20:10), which became a reality in May 1948. The Lord stated that the generation who sees religious Israel come alive again (symbolically represented in leaves on the tree, but no fruit – Luke 13:6-9), would see the coming of the Lord. An accompanying sign was the birth of many new nations (pictured in the appearance of many trees). The Jewish Levitical System has not yet returned at the time of this writing, but it will, in accordance with the testimony of Jesus Christ. When Christ returns to establish His kingdom on earth, the nation of Israel will be restored, and the Holy Spirit will indwell them. For this reason spiritual Israel is symbolized by an olive tree in Scripture (Zech. 4:1-7, Rom. 11:17). Pertaining to Israel, the vine, the fig tree and the olive tree are quite distinctive symbols.

Luke provides a wide angle snapshot of the **Gentile political system of the day**. The other Gospel writers mostly ignore these details. For example, Luke informs us that Augustus was Caesar and Quirinius was governor of Syria at the time of Christ's birth (Luke 2:1-2). When Christ began His ministry at thirty years of age, Tiberius was Ceasar, and Pontius Pilate was governor of Judea (Luke 3:1). After disclosing the names and offices of Gentile authorities, he then documents those Jewish civil and religious leaders who served under Gentile rule: Herod, Philip and Lysanias were tetrarchs, and Annas and Caiaphas were high priests (Luke 3:1-2).

# The Personal Element

In Matthew, a star guided the magi, and Joseph received all divine direction through the impersonal medium of dreams. Not so in Luke's account. An angel appeared to Zacharias while he was performing his priestly duties in the holy place of the temple. The two of them engaged in a face to face discussion, and the angel provided prophetic revelation concerning John the Baptist and the coming Messiah to Zacharias. This communication was all done through normal speech. Because Zacharias sought a sign to validate the message, he was smitten mute by the angel until after John's birth. Apparently, there are both advantages and disadvantages to direct personal communication with God's angels.

In the same chapter, the angel Gabriel speaks with Mary in her own home concerning the conception and birth of the Messiah. The home setting, the personal greeting (from an angel who identifies himself by name), and the tender dialogue entreats human sentiment to fully identify with the scene. Whether it be through the voices of Zacharias, Anna, Simeon, individual angelic messengers, or an angelic host praising God on a hillside, divine announcements to mankind are much more personal and less aloof in Luke than they are in Matthew.

Luke often is more specific in identifying the humanness of key characters associated with Christ's miracles and teachings than the other Gospel writers. Two examples will suffice to demonstrate this tendency. In the account of the healing of the leper, Luke specifically notes that *"a man full of leprosy"* came to Christ (Luke 5:12). Matthew, however, describing the same incident wrote, *"there came a leper" (Matt. 8:2).* In the healing of the demon possessed man, Luke states, *"there met Him* ***a certain man*** *from the city who had demons for a long time" (Luke 8:27, NKJV)*, but Matthew refers to this man by using the pronoun "he" instead of the more familiar and personal identification (Matt. 8:28).

## Outline

Luke's Gospel is less chronological than Mark's and John's, but perhaps more systematic in presentation than any of the Gospel accounts. Like Matthew, Luke contains a distinct shift in the Lord's ministry after His transfiguration. David

Gooding highlights the natural twofold advance of Luke's presentation of Christ:

> Luke's inspired presentation of Christ is arranged in two great movements: first the 'Coming' of the Lord from heaven to earth; and then His 'Going' from earth to heaven. The turning point between them stands at chapter 9 verse 51. An unforgettable scene marks the beginning of the 'Coming': when Mary and Joseph arrive in Bethlehem to have their names registered in the census lists of the world empire, there is no room in the inn for the world's Saviour to be born. Nonetheless the 'Coming' ends in glory: at the transfiguration, Christ appears supreme and central in the coming universal kingdom of God. An equally unforgettable scene marks the beginning of the 'Going' (see Luke 9:51-56): certain Samaritans refuse to receive Him into their village.... Appropriately, the climax of the 'Going' shows the man, Jesus, rejected and crucified on the earth, but now risen and ascending, being received up into glory.[3]

## Key Words

As mentioned previously, Luke stresses the title theme of *"Son of Man"* in his Gospel to distinctly focus his audience on the humanity of Christ and how He related to mankind in fulfilling His sacrificial mission. The Lord Jesus was born to suffer and die. For comparison, Luke refers to this title twenty-five times, while John has twelve occurrences.

Another key phrase in Luke is *"all the people."* It is found twice in Matthew, thrice in Mark, and once in John, but eleven times in Luke. In His birth and in His baptism, He was identified with *"all the people."* Frequently in His preaching and in His miracles, He was identified with *"all the people."* The writer of Hebrews states that He *"tasted death for every man" (Heb. 2:9).* He was truly a man of the people and for *"all the people."*

Matthew wrote of the *"Kingdom of Heaven"* thirty-three times in his Gospel, while only referring to the *"Kingdom of God"* five times. Luke is nearly opposite this representation with thirty-three occurrences of the *"Kingdom of God"* and no mention of the *"Kingdom of Heaven."* Certainly, the hierarchical presentation of Christ as king, versus a man, cascades into the decision of submission. The *"Kingdom of Heaven"* presents a choice, whereas the *"Kingdom of God"* more closely acknowledges man's dependence upon a sovereign God. The Lord told the Jews that the *"Kingdom of God"* was in the midst of them, but they did not recognize it; therefore, it would not come visibly but would continue in its invisible spiritual form until Christ's Second Advent to the earth (Luke 17:20-21).

Four key words in Luke clearly express the manifold purpose of the Father sending His Son to planet earth. Through Christ, God would **bless** mankind with **mercy**, **peace**, and **joy**.

| Term | Matthew | Mark | Luke | John |
|------|---------|------|------|------|
| Blessed (Bless) | 19 | 7 | 30 | 2 |
| Peace | 9 | 2 | 10 | 0 |
| Mercy | 6 | 8 | 19 | 6 |
| Joy | 6 | 0 | 11 | 8 |
| **Total** | **40** | **17** | **70** | **16** |

## The Son of Man

Who better than a physician to speak of the humanity of Christ? Not only does Luke show us the moral beauty and perfection of Christ, but he also reveals to us the frailties of His humanness. Luke presents to us a touchable Saviour, who desires to touch others with compassion and kindness.

"The Son of Man" is an Old Testament term to express human association and, thus, links Christ to earth as a man. As stated in the previous section, Luke applies the title to the Lord Jesus twenty-five times in his Gospel, while, in contrast, John, whose theme is the deity of Christ, only refers to the Lord as the Son of Man twelve times. The Lord Jesus spoke more often of Himself as *"the Son of Man"* than as *"the Son of God,"* for the title identified His mission and not His essence. It is noted that only the Lord Jesus speaks of Himself as *"the Son of Man"* in the Gospels, some eighty-four times; yet, there are fourteen references to "others" identifying the Lord Jesus as the *"Son of God,"* a title He applies to Himself only five times (all occurrences are rightly placed in John). The Lord normally spoke of His humble station and ministry, while others were privileged to acknowledge His divine rule and essence.

One of the early references in the Bible to the *"Son of Man"* is found in Psalm 8. This Psalm is then quoted in the epistle to the Hebrews and applied to speak of the incarnation of Christ. The title *"Son of Man"* is not found in any New Testament epistle, except for the one reference in Hebrews 2:6-9, which refers to Psalm 8. The epistles are books of wisdom given to the Church to understand the great mysteries of God, which were before hidden in the recesses of God's mind. The Church, in Christ, has a heavenly, not an earthly, calling. The Lord Jesus will always be a man, but now He is highly exalted and at the right hand of God in heaven. It would not be inappropriate to address Him personally as the *"Son of Man."* This is why the expression is not found in the epistles, save once in Hebrews as an explanation of Psalm 8. Christ finished that mission to earth, and consequently, at the pleasure of the Father, now has a name above all names.

# The "Only Begotten" Son

The term "begotten" means "unique." The writer of Hebrews refers to Isaac being Abraham's *"only begotten son" (Heb. 11:17)*, but Abraham obviously had other sons. Ishmael was born 13 years before Isaac, and several sons were born to Abraham through Keturah after the death of Abraham's first wife, Sarah (Gen. 25:1-4). But Isaac was Abraham's **only son** of promise; through Isaac, and him alone, would the Messiah come, and God's covenant with Abraham be fulfilled.

The term "begotten" is specifically connected with the Lord Jesus in three ways in Scripture to declare some facet of "uniqueness." He is the only begotten of the Father (John 1:14; 1:18; 3:16; 3:18), which speaks of the Son's unique position and eternal relationship as the Son of God, the One who was with the Father in glory from the beginning (John 1:1; 17:5). You cannot have an *"Everlasting Father"* without an "Everlasting Son" (Isa. 9:6). This is John's perspective of Christ.

Then, in Hebrews 1:6, the term "begotten" is applied to the Son's incarnation. J. N. Darby comments to the divine glories associated with the twofold offices of Christ in Hebrews 1:

> This glory is twofold, and in connection with the twofold office of Christ. It is the divine glory of the Person of the Messiah, the Son of God. The solemn authority of His word is connected with this glory. And then there is the glory with which His humanity is invested according to the counsels of God – the glory of the Son of man; a glory connected with His sufferings and in all the temptations to which the saints, whose nature He had assumed, are subjected.[4]

> *"Thou art my Son, this day have I begotten thee."* It is this character of Sonship, proper to the Messiah, which, as a real relationship, distinguishes Him. He was from eternity the Son of the Father; but it is not precisely in this point of view that He

is here considered. The name expresses the same relationship, but it is to the Messiah born on earth that this title is here applied.[5]

"Begotten" is also used to speak of Christ's unique resurrection and ascent back to glory in Hebrews 1:5 and Acts 13:33. Paul declares that Christ is *"the first fruits"* from the dead (1 Cor. 15:20) – the first to experience glorification. Christ is merely the wave sheaf; the full harvest is yet to come. The hope of resurrection is the *"blessed hope"* for every true believer (Tit. 2:13). All of the Gospel writers declare the resurrection glory of Christ. The Son of God is "unique" in all three of these facets: His eternality, incarnation and resurrection. Luke focuses our attention on the unique humanity of Christ resulting directly from the incarnation.

## The Glories of Christ

The glories of the Lord Jesus are threefold: Intrinsic, Official, and Moral. His intrinsic glory is that which is essential to Him as the Son of God – He is fully divine and an equal to the Father: *"O Father, glorify Thou Me with Thine own self with the glory which I had with Thee before the world was" (John 17:5).*

Christ's official glory is that which pertains to Him as the Mediator of the New Covenant – He is the Great High Priest. The Lord acquired His official glory; His reward and promotion for finishing the immeasurable work of redemption assigned to Him: *"Father, I will that they also, whom Thou hast given Me, be with Me where I am, that they may behold my glory, which Thou hast given Me" (John 17:24).*

The Lord's moral glory consists of the perfections which characterize His earthly life and ministry: *"And the Word was made flesh, and dwelt among us (and we beheld His glory, the glory as of the only begotten of the Father), full of grace and truth" (John 1:14).* He was perfect in all His doings, in every circumstance, in each word spoken, and in every thought mentally conceived.

During His earthly sojourn, His intrinsic glory was veiled and His official glory not yet received. However, His moral glory could not be hid; His character shined forth the integrity and perfections of His divine essence. Of this glory A. W. Tozer wrote, "Christ is God acting like God in the lowly raiments of human flesh."[6] It is His moral glory which was witnessed by man and illuminates every page of the Gospel accounts.

William G. Moorehead speaks to the moral glory evident in the Lord's humanity:

> The moral glory of Jesus appears in His development as Son of Man. The nature which He assumed was our nature, sin and sinful propensities only excepted. His was a real and a true humanity, one which must pass through the various stages of growth like any other member of the race. From infancy to youth, from youth to manhood, there was steady increase both of His bodily powers and mental faculties; but the progress was orderly. "No unhealthy precocity marked the holiest of infancies." He was first a child, and afterwards a man, not a man in child's years.

> As Son of Man He was compassed about with all the sinless infirmities that belong to our nature. He has needs common to all; need of food, of rest, of human sympathy and of divine assistance. He is subject to Joseph and Mary, He is a worshiper in the synagogue and the Temple; He weeps over the guilty and hardened city, and at the grave of a loved one; He expresses His dependence on God by prayer.

> Nothing is more certain than that the Gospel narratives present the Lord Jesus as a true man.... At every stage of His development, in every relation of life, in every part of His

service He is absolutely perfect. To no part of His life does a mistake attach, over no part of it does a cloud rest, nowhere is there defect.[7]

## The Unique Conception and Birth of Christ

What are miracles? Everything mankind has observed in creation he has sought to characterize by rules of order. Conservation of energy and motion, laws of gravity and thermodynamics and the like represent our knowledge of creation based on observation. Therefore, God has to cause some non-regularities in our ordered world in order to call our attention to the fact that there is an outside influence to be reckoned with – the Creator.

Such were the births of Isaac, John the Baptist, and Jesus Christ. Before each miracle (an irregularity in an ordered system) occurred, Scripture records that the people understood the natural order that was in place. These were not ignorant people. They knew how babies were made and when procreation could no longer happen. If they had not known these things, no miracle would have been recognized, and God would have received no glory in doing it. In the case of Sarah and Elizabeth, they both were past menopause and physically incapable of bearing children (Gen. 18:11; Luke 1:18, 36). In the case of Mary, the mother of Jesus, she was a virgin (Luke 1:34). So, it is really thanks to science that we have the wherewithal to actually recognize the hand of God in our lives! Without the understanding of order, we would not be able to recognize a miracle when one occurs. Luke is very careful to document the "order" of things, so we might better recognize the divine miracle of the incarnation of Christ.

The conception and birth of the Lord Jesus was "unique." There is no patient confidentiality in this matter; Luke provides a full medical report for all to read:

1. The conception of Christ was through the power of the Holy Spirit (Luke 1:35).
2. The conception of Christ did not involve any man (Luke 1:34).
3. The conception of Christ took place in the womb; normally, conception occurs in the fallopian tubes and then the embryo later attaches to the womb (Luke 1:31).
4. The conception of Christ would never be repeated again, for the Lord Jesus, the Last Adam, need only suffer once for sin (Heb. 10:10-18), and He would rule over the house of Israel *forever* (Luke 1:33).
5. The conception of Christ resulted in a virgin giving birth to *"the Son of the Highest" (Luke 1:27; 1:32; 1:34).*

The first three humans to walk upon this planet entered the world in different ways: Adam became a living soul after God breathed a spirit into a heap of dust gathered from the earth. Eve was created from materials taken from Adam's side. Cain was a product of human procreation. The Lord Jesus entered the world by a fourth means, a virgin birth. The means by which one enters the world does not determine if one is human or not, for Adam, Eve, Cain and Jesus Christ were all human, but Christ was of a different spiritual nature than any other, for He did not come from Adam.

## The Unique Humanity of Christ

Satan was defeated at Calvary (John 12:31) and further humiliated at the resurrection of Christ (Eph. 1:19-21). His only recourse since those triumphant events has been to cast doubt upon the work of Christ and to defame His person and character. Satan and his worldly domain hate the Lord Jesus and will go to any extreme to slander Him and to discourage and frustrate those who desire to live for Christ (John 15:18-19). Any teaching which undermines the divine person and the moral perfection of Christ is an attack at the very foundation of the Christian faith; if no flawless Christ, if no divine nature – then no salvation. The Lord Jesus said, *"if you do not believe that I am [He], you will die in your sins" (John 8:24, NKJV)*. Note: *He* in the "I am" statement is not in the Greek text.

There are various erroneous teachings concerning the person of Christ. Some say Christ is not fully God, nor fully man. Others teach that Christ became some hybrid creature, a created being, between God and man, but neither God nor man. This view, commonly held among many cults today, is one that Paul confronts in the book of Colossians. Yet, others see a schizophrenic Jesus, someone with a dual personality, who switches back and forth in personality and natures. Christ is not diminished deity added to a human personality; God literally and personally became a human, without emptying Himself of any divine attributes (John 1:14). This issue will be discussed more thoroughly in the study of John's Gospel.

*"Great is the mystery of Godliness. God was manifest in the flesh" (1 Tim. 3:16)*. Christ was fully man, but He had a unique human nature, different from our nature. Because there is no definite article in the Greek before "flesh," this verse is better rendered, as John Darby translates it, *"God has been manifested in flesh."* [8] God was manifest "in flesh," not "in the flesh." The Lord Jesus was veiled in flesh (Heb. 10:20); He was made flesh (John 1:14) but was not in the flesh – the nature of His flesh did not rule Him; it served Him. His flesh had not been invaded by the corruption of sin. A. W. Tozer put it this way, "Christ is God acting like God in the lowly raiments of human flesh." [9]

Paul explains the difference: *"What the law could not do in that it was weak through **the flesh**, God sending His own Son **in** *the likeness of sinful flesh" (Rom. 8:3)*. The same Greek word *homoioma,* translated as "likeness" in this verse, is also applied in Philippians 2:7, which states that Christ *"was made in the likeness of men."* The word "likeness" in both verses means "resemblance" or "form." Humanly speaking, His form was that of a man, but He was more; He also possessed a divine nature. The Lord looked like everyone else, but He didn't act like everyone else. His life was unique for *"in Him is no sin" (1 Jn. 3:5)*; He *"knew no sin" (2 Cor. 5:21)*; and He *"did no sin" (1 Pet. 2:22)*.

Speaking of Christ, the writer of Hebrews declares the matter frankly, *"who **being the brightness of His** [God's] **glory,** and **the express image of His** [God's] **person,** and upholding all things by the word of His power, when He had by Himself purged our sins, sat down on the right hand of the Majesty on high" (Heb. 1:3)*. It was needful for Christ to be veiled in flesh, or mankind would have been consumed by the direct presence of Almighty God. The veil of flesh allowed Christ to outshine the direct moral glory of God to the World. J. B. Phillips wrote: "Christ is the aperture through which the immensity and magnificence of God can be seen." [10] When you looked upon the Lord Jesus, you would see the form of a man, with the character of God shining through. Mark the words of Christ to Philip:

> *Philip said to Him, "Lord, show us the Father, and it is sufficient for us." Jesus said to him, "Have I been with you so long, and yet you have not known Me, Philip? He who has seen Me has seen the Father; so how can you say, 'Show us the Father'? Do you not believe that I am in the Father, and the Father in Me? The words that I speak to you I do not speak on My own authority; but the Father who dwells in Me does the works" (John 14:8-10, NKJV).*

As stated previously, Christ was fully human but had a different spiritual nature than Adam. According to Ecclesiastes 7:29, Adam was made "upright" or "innocent." Until Adam sinned, he reflected the character of God, for he bore God's image and likeness (Gen. 1:26). Adam was God's representative of Himself in creation before the fall of man (Heb. 2:6-8). After Adam had sinned, he no longer bore the likeness of God, but his own likeness (Gen. 5:3). The Last Adam, Christ, was not just **innocent humanity**, as Adam was; He was **holy humanity** (Luke 1:35). *"For in Him dwelleth all the fullness of the Godhead bodily" (Col. 2:9)*. Nowhere in Scripture do we read of Adam being "holy." God was not in Adam, but *"God was in Christ, reconciling the world unto Himself" (2 Cor. 5:19)*.

When Adam sinned, he made a transition from **innocent humanity** to **condemned humanity** and was cursed by God. Everyone coming from Adam is condemned as well (Rom. 5:12-14). Through the obedience of Christ came the offer of grace, forgiveness and restoration (Rom. 5:15-21). Those who respond to the Gospel of Christ become **redeemed humanity** and wait to become **glorified humanity** at Christ's return to the air (1 Thess. 4:13-18). This moment will be the culmination of our salvation; we will be saved from the presence of sin through the transforming power of God. Sin will no longer dwell within our members, for we will have Christ's sinless nature (Phil. 3:21). The work that started with regeneration will be complete, and the believer will be instantly and fully conformed to the image of Christ (Rom. 8:29). What Adam lost is fully restored through the Last Adam, the Lord Jesus.

*Being confident of this very thing, that He which hath begun a good work in you will perform it until the day of Jesus Christ (Phil. 1:6).*

We understand that Christ, as **holy humanity**, could not sin, for there was nothing in His members that would respond to sin; His very essence repulsed sin and loathed its working. Some have suggested that the external solicitations of Satan upon the Lord Jesus caused some internal moral struggle within His person. This is not the case. How could the Father, looking down from heaven, declare, *"This is my beloved Son, in whom I am well pleased" (Matt. 3:17),* if the Lord was struggling internally with thoughts of sin. As John declared, the Lord Jesus **was**, not might be, *"the Lamb of God, which taketh away the sin of the world" (John 1:29).* The Father never questioned the impeccability of Christ – only Satan and men do that – He was blameless and perfect, the only acceptable substitutional sacrifice for man's sin.

Scripturally speaking, the word "temptation" has different meanings depending upon the context of the related passage. The book of James informs us of three prominent meanings of "testing." The word *peirasmos,* normally translated as *"temptation"* in the KJV, may also be translated as "trial" or "testing." *Peirasmos* has the meaning of "demonstrating the proof of something" either through difficult experience or solicitation.

**Holy Trials**
1. *My brethren, count it all joy when you fall into various **trials**, knowing that the **testing** of your faith produces patience (Jas. 1:2-3, NKJV)... Blessed is the man who endures **temptation**; for when he has been **approved**, he will receive the crown of life which the Lord has promised to those who love Him (Jas. 1:12, NKJV).*

### Unholy Temptations

1. *Let no one say when he is **tempted**, "I am tempted by God;" for God cannot be tempted by evil, nor does He Himself tempt anyone. But each one is tempted **when he is drawn away by his own desires and enticed**. Then, when **desire has conceived**, it gives birth to sin; and sin, when it is full-grown, brings forth death (Jas. 1:13-15, NKJV).*

2. *Submit yourselves therefore to God. **Resist the devil**, and he will flee from you (Jas. 4:7).*

The Lord Jesus knows all about being tested through sufferings; in fact, the writer of Hebrews states His full maturity was demonstrated in this manner (Heb. 2:10). He also is quite familiar with the latter form of testing, for on one occasion Satan externally solicited Him to do evil for forty days straight (Mark 1:13). He did not respond to Satan's temptations or falter in character through life's difficulties.

The second form of temptation the Lord Jesus knows nothing about (drawn away by internal desires)! This is the pragmatic lusting of our fallen members – the lusts from within. John tells us that sin was an intruder into humanity; it was not inherent in Adam, but it entered in from the world and then passed down to the next generation. *"For all that is in the world, the lust of the flesh, and the lust of the eyes, and the pride of life, is not of the Father, but is of the world (1 Jn. 2:16).* The ungodly lusting of our members originally came from the world.

The basis of lusting is dissatisfaction. Ever since Satan told Eve that she could be more than what God had created her to be and have more than what God had given her, humanity has been dissatisfied. Dissatisfaction advocates that "God is unfairly limiting me, and I desire more." Is it possible for Christ to have been dissatisified? No, Christ, being God, is perfectly satisfied – He is self-sufficient. Lusting "in the flesh" is not of God, but of the world. Adam and Eve ate because they were told they could have more than what they presently had. Satan sinned because he was dissatisfied with being an anointed cherub and wanted the throne. But no evil desires were a part of Christ's humanity. We have difficulty understanding this fact because we have ungodly lusting in our flesh.

Jesus Christ: the condescension of divinity and the exaltation of humanity.

— Phillips Brooks

## Unique Priesthood of Christ

In His role as Son of Man, the Lord holds two offices: Priest and Prophet. *"Wherefore, holy brethren, partakers of the heavenly calling, consider the Apostle and High Priest of our profession, Christ Jesus"* (Heb. 3:1). As Prophet, or Apostle, He is the sent One from the Father to perfectly represent God to mankind. As Priest, Christ perfectly represents man to God. The writer of Hebrews informs us why Christ must be the Son of Man to be our High Priest:

> *For every high priest **taken from among men** is ordained for men in things pertaining to God, that he may offer both gifts and sacrifices for sins: Who can have **compassion on the ignorant**, and on them that are out of the way; for that **he himself also is compassed with infirmity** (Heb. 5:1-2).*

Christ being **holy humanity**, demonstrated compassion for others and felt the infirmities of mankind, yet **sin apart**. After His resurrection, Christ experienced glorification. Presently, He is not only **holy humanity** but **glorified humanity.** The writer of Hebrews informs us that Christ presently sits at the right hand of God (Heb. 1:3) and is ever occupied with making intercession on our behalf – He is our Great High Priest (Heb. 2:17 and 4:15). Having a distorted or deficient view of Christ's humanity ensures a degraded view of His priestly operations and sympathies. It would be a natural tendency for us, with a fallen nature, to approach and solicit Christ for help and comfort concerning depraved vexations which He can neither relate to nor assist with.

> *For we have not an high priest which cannot be touched with the feeling of our infirmities; but was in all points tempted like as [we are, yet], without sin (Heb. 4:15).* Note: *"we are, yet"* is not in the Greek text.

J. N. Darby translates the passage in the literal sense and without the translator's additional words, which distract from the purest meaning of the text.

> *For we have not a high priest not able to sympathize with our infirmities, but tempted in all things in like manner, **sin apart** (Heb. 4:15).*[11]

The latter portion of this verse has been used to teach that Christ was tested and did not sin. Though this is true, it is not what the writer is declaring. The passage is not highlighting the sinless perfection of Christ but His inherent impeccability. Christ was tested in every way you and I are, **except in our sin – His members were sin apart**. Jeremiah bluntly summarizes our internal spiritual condition: *"The heart is deceitful above all things, and desperately wicked" (Jer. 17:9).* Our members are prone to sin because we are rotten to the core! Modern day Christianity has generally accepted this passage to mean what it does not say, but this was not the case of believers before our time – they understood that Christ was both sinless and impeccable in character. Read and appreciate the insights into Christ's humanity and priesthood from some brethren who have long since been with the Lord:

William Newell clarifies the meaning of Hebrews 4:15:

The word "yet" inserted in both the Authorized and the Revised versions here, "yet without sin," is an utter hindrance, instead of a true translation. The Greek reads, "tempted like as we, without sin," or, "sin apart." The Greek word for without, *choris*, signifies having no connection with, no relationship to. Temptation does not involve sin.[12]

With the understanding that Christ had no connection with or relationship to sin in His members, Harry Ironside puts the whole verse into proper perspective:

Our High Priest then is not One whose heart is indifferent to our circumstances; not One who cannot be touched with the feeling of our infirmities. He is as truly human as we, and in the days of His flesh He was tempted in all points like ourselves, though apart from sin. The expression, "yet without sin," has frequently been taken to mean, "yet without sinning," as though it simply implied that He did not fail when exposed to temptation, but the exact rendering would be "sin apart." That is, His temptations were entirely from without. He was never tempted by inbred sin as we are. He could say, *"The prince of this world cometh and hath nothing in Me."* When we are tempted from without, we have a traitor within who ever seeks to open the door of the citadel to the enemy. But it was otherwise with Him. If any ask, How then could His temptations be as real as ours? Let us remember that when temptation was first presented to Adam and Eve, they were sinless beings, but being merely human, they yielded and plunged the race into ruin and disaster. Christ was not only innocent but holy, for He was God as well as Man.[13]

John Darby explains the practical side of relating to Christ as High Priest:

He has, in all things, been tempted like ourselves, sin apart; so that he can sympathize with our infirmities. The word brings to light the intents of the heart, judges the will, and all that has not God for its object and its source. Then, as far as weakness is concerned, we have His sympathy. Christ of course had no evil desires: He was tempted in every way, apart from sin. Sin had no part in it at all. But I do not wish for sympathy with the sin that is in me; I detest it, I wish it to be mortified – judged unsparingly. This the word does. For my weakness and my difficulties I seek sympathy; and I find it in the priesthood of Christ.[14]

How does Christ, as holy humanity and our High Priest, feel our infirmities? F. W. Bruce explains:

How great an encouragement to know that upon the throne of God there is One who can be "touched by the feelings of our infirmities, but was in all things tempted like as we are, sin apart." Sin was to Him no temptation: there was nothing within that answered to it, except in suffering. There was and could be with Him no sinful infirmity; but He was true Man, His divine nature taking nothing from the verity of His manhood, living a dependent life as we, and, with no callousness such as the flesh in us produces, in a world everywhere racked with suffering through sin, and out of joint, the trial of which He knew as no other could.[15]

William Kelly nicely summarizes the entire matter of Christ's humanity and associated priesthood:

> We are too familiar with the human and selfish argument that He could not sympathize with us adequately if exempt from those internal and evil workings, bemoaned in Romans 7 and bitterly known by every soul born of God, at least in the early days of his awakening. But if we needed the Lord to be similarly harassed in order to feel fully with us, we should on that ground want Him to have yielded, as we alas – have often done, in order to sympathize with us in our sad failures. No! That ground is wretchedly and absolutely opposed to Christ; and what the word reveals as the remedy for evil within and without in every form and degree is not Christ's sympathy, but His propitiatory suffering for us. He sympathizes with us in our holy, not in our unholy, temptations. For our unholiness He died; the cross alone has met it fully in God's sight. Had there been in fact the least inward taint of sin, His sensibility of evil had been impaired, his sufferings diminished, and His sympathy hindered, to say nothing of the deadly wound to His person, unfitted by such an evil nature to be a sacrifice for sin.[16]

Christ, as a man, sustained the harsh living conditions of a cursed planet, the contradiction of sinners, the opposition of Satan, and the hatred of the World. As High Priest, Christ is in no way sympathizing with sin or forbidden desires but with the suffering saints of God as they endure what He already has but in no way to the extent that He did. He knows all about living for God in a wicked world. In this we find a solace and comfort for our distressed souls. But there is no pity at the Throne of Grace for the lusting of our flesh and the active sin of our members, for these must be dealt a deadly blow from the sword of the Spirit. Christ weeps not at the funeral of rotting and vile flesh. If it were our lusting and sin He was sympathizing with, He would be sympathetic with all men and not just believers. Yet, only the redeemed are invited to *"come boldly,"* and only the redeemed *"obtain mercy, and find grace to help in time of need" (Heb. 4:16).*

Beloved of the Lord, let us not degrade Him in character or His priestly office by thinking of Him in some way tolerant, considerate or sympathetic to matters that are foreign to His being and are repulsive to His holy nature! He experientially understands the consequences of our sin but not our propensity to embrace it.

As Andrew Jukes exclaims, the Lord Jesus is God's perfect man:

> Here is man according to God, the pattern Man, in and through whom man is blessed and God glorified, seen not only in moral perfectness, but in all the sufferings and honors, which according to God's purpose are the heritage of the sons of men; first humbled into the dust of death, then exalted to God's right hand, His image and likeness, to rule as Lord of all.[17]

When one gazed upon the Lord Jesus Christ, all the moral perfection and splendor of the Father was evidenced. Only the Lord Jesus could legitimately declare, *"He that hath seen Me hath seen the Father" (John 14:9).*

# The Life of Christ

There was a reason that the widely acclaimed "Jesus" film was based solely on the Gospel of Luke. The good doctor provides more details of the life of Christ than any other Gospel writer and does so with a style that, humanly speaking, is both interesting and appealing. Luke shows a Saviour who relates to and serves mankind. Christ's compassion, emotions, and limitations of humanity are interwoven throughout. Luke, like no other writer, informs us of the Lord's human distinctives: fatigue, exhaustion, thirst, hunger, sleep, or the lack thereof, talking, walking, listening, etc. In so doing, Luke introduces to his audience a real and tangible Saviour.

The four Gospels in no way provide a complete account of the Lord's ministry. John poetically asserts this reality at the close of his Gospel: *"And there are also many other things which Jesus did, the which, if they should be written every one, I suppose that even the world itself could not contain the books that should be written" (John 21:25).* Of what the Gospels do record, we understand that Christ had a very full and prosperous ministry, which included teaching, miracles, and prayer. Matthew provides a concise statement, *"And Jesus went about all Galilee, teaching in their synagogues, and preaching the Gospel of the kingdom, and healing all manner of sickness and all manner of disease among the people" (Matt. 4:23).*

The teaching ministry of Christ was quite diverse in format and audience focus. Only two public messages are recorded in detail. "The Sermon on the Mount" was lengthy and was presented to a mixed group of believers, seekers and opposers, near the beginning of Christ's three-year-plus public ministry. The last, the "Seven Woes" message, was directed to the Pharisees at the end of His ministry. Between these two messages is a vast amount of personal instruction, mainly to His disciples. Christ would entrust His continuing work and the future of the kingdom into their hands; they had to be prepared for it. The disciples could not be faithful to the Lord's command, *"teach all nations... to observe all things whatsoever I have commanded you,"* if they didn't understand what the Lord taught. The Lord preached the Gospel wherever He went, but the bulk of His teaching ministry was intended for His disciples. By example, the Lord showed us that He planned to build His church through personal discipleship. The remainder of the Lord's public teaching ministry is presented in the parables He told and in the personal instruction provided while performing miracles.

## Christ's Parables

The Lord's parables are one of the most mystifying aspects of the Lord's ministry. He told some forty parables in all. On the surface, these parables are often perplexing, cryptic, and hard to understand. The Lord told parables in response to questions, self-righteous attitudes, pious murmurings or as a means of engaging an audience to think about spiritual matters. On some occasions, the subject matter was so vast that the Lord strung several parables together in addressing His listeners, but at other times, a single allegory sufficed to portray the intended meaning.

If studied individually, these forty parables seem to address a wide range of subjects and have an equally vast intended purpose. Yet, stepping back from the intrinsic value of each story to a panoramic view, the Lord's parable ministry reveals some interesting patterns. For example, it can be surmised from the collective Gospel accounts that the Lord told no parables for perhaps a year and a half after His baptism. Further observation reveals that the Lord spoke only fourteen parables by the close of the Galilean Ministry and that eight of the fourteen were told on one day by the seashore of Galilee. It was not uncommon for several months to past without any parables being communicated or for several to be spoken all at once. Again viewing the Gospel accounts collectively, all the parables seem to be spoken on only 15 different occasions. Interestingly, fifteen of the forty parables were conveyed on two occasions. It is also observed that nearly two-thirds of the parables were disclosed in the last seven or eight months of the Lord's ministry on earth.

What is a parable? The word "parable" literally means to "cast along side". The Lord used a story format to align (cast along side) a spiritual truth with a common every day activity the people could relate to, such as sowing seed, using a dragnet for fishing, or watching birds feed in a mustard tree. Arthur Pink affords us a simple and concise definition of a parable:

> The popular definition of Christ's parables is that they were earthly stories with a heavenly meaning. How man gets things upside down! The truth is, that His parables were heavenly stories with an earthly meaning, having to do with His earthly people, in earthly connections.[1]

Why did the Lord speak in parables? The Lord Jesus intentionally spoke in parables to reveal truth, yet in a partially-veiled manner. The parables were not just enjoyable stories but served as a test to the hearers. The casual onlooker, the "window shopper," would hear and not understand, nor would he or she desire any more understanding – "thanks for the good story." But those longing to understand the spiritual significance of the parable would seek the Lord for further instruction – this was often just the disciples.

As the Lord approached the cross, the parable veil thinned, and the meanings became more obvious, even to the dissident. While speaking parables in Jerusalem on the Tuesday before His death, even the Pharisees understood that He was speaking of them. In general, the parables can be organized into four main subjects, with each compilation of parables leading to the next in a nearly chronological fashion. These are:

> The "Mystery of the Kingdom" parables,
> Salvation and the Fruit Thereof parables,
> Second Advent and Jewish Attitudes parables,
> Rewarding the Faithful parables.

In the eight "Mystery of the Kingdom" parables, the Lord reveals a chronology of events that would characterize the *"Kingdom of Heaven"* from His first advent (a seed sowing mission) until His return to rule the world in peace. Satan is busy in the first four parables undermining the Kingdom of Heaven (the realm of human profession of God's sovereignty). In these parables, Satan is seen attacking the Gospel message, trying to neutralize the influence of believers on earth, corrupting Church leadership, order, and structure, and finally, promoting false doctrine within the Church. However, in the last three parables, Satan is absent, and God demonstrates His fathomless grace in saving sinners. Christ paid the great price for the hidden treasure (yet unrestored Israel) and the pearl (the Church) and also effects blessing for those Gentiles living through the tribulation period who did not bow to the anti-Christ or receive his mark.

In the second group of parables, the Lord focuses on important aspects of salvation such as not mixing the law with grace and the necessity of repentance to receive salvation. Then several parables reinforce the "practice" of the believer once his "position" in Christ is secure: forgiving one another, giving unselfishly, loving others, obeying the word, understanding the cost of being a disciple, and returning love to the Lord.

The remaining parables largely focus on the Lord's Second Advent and were mainly told in the final three or four months of the Lord's ministry on earth. Part of these parables focus on religious pride and Jewish rejection of the Lord and the consequences of that rejection, while others emphasize rewards for the faithful when the Lord comes into His Kingdom. In "The Wicked Servant" parable, the Lord punctuates the importance that believers be "future thinking" and "invest in eternity" and not in a world under judgment. He then informs believers that He will reward them fairly according to how faithful they were to "opportunities to serve" (parable of the Laborers), "abilities given" (the parable of the Talents) and "yielded availability" (the parable of the Pounds).

## Christ's Miracles

*"Ye men of Israel, hear these words; Jesus of Nazareth, a man approved of God among you by miracles and wonders and signs, which God did by Him in the midst of you, as ye yourselves also know" (Acts 2:22).* On the day of Pentecost, Peter emphatically proclaimed that the miracles Christ did were of God and a sign for them of the fulfillment of Scripture – Jesus Christ was the promised Messiah.

Apparently, only a fraction of the total number of Christ's miracles were written down for our appreciation. Mark notes,

*"For He had healed many; insomuch that they pressed upon Him for to touch Him, as many as had plagues"* (Mark 3:10). The following summarizes the types of miracles that were recorded:

**Miracles of Physical Healing.** Included are healings of fever (2), blindness (4), hemorrhage (1), dropsy (1), leprosy (2), paralysis (4), deaf-mute (1), and severed body parts (1).

**Miracles of Resurrection.** It is worthy to note that only three resurrections were recorded in the Old Testament; Elijah and Elisha accomplished these. The Lord raised three people from the dead during His ministry on earth, then effected His own resurrection also (John 10:17-18). The Lord Jesus was the seventh and, thus, the perfect resurrection of the Bible.

**Miracles Related to Demon Possession.** The Lord is recorded seven different times as driving out demons from the host they possessed. In each case, being freed from demon possession brought emotional and physical healing.

**Miracles Related to Earthly Physics.** Besides miracles that brought personal healing, the Lord Jesus performed supernatural feats to demonstrate His power over creation. Twice He calmed a raging storm by a simple command. Water became His sidewalk for crossing the Sea of Galilee and for Peter's brief excursion as well. Directly after this event, the Lord instantaneously moved their boat a great distance across the sea to arrive at Capernaun.

**Miracles Related to Plant and Animal Life.** Though the Lord had no tax liability, He graciously agreed to pay taxes so as to not stumble the unsaved. For this reason, and for this purpose only, Peter received the money via the mouth of a fish. On two different occasions, the Lord commanded fishermen to drop their nets for a great draught of fish. Near the end of the Lord's ministry, to demonstrate His disgust for fruitless Israel, He cursed a fig tree. The disciples noted the next day that it was completely withered.

**Miracles Related to Food and Drink.** On two different occasions, the Lord took a few fish and loaves of bread and multiplied them to feed thousands of people to their fill. In so doing, He demonstrated that He was the Master of quantity. The Lord's first miracle, turning water into the best wine, confirmed Him to be the Master of quality. He is both willing and able to share all that He has and the best that He has with those who will trust Him.

# Christ's Prayer Life

As in Mark, Luke portrays the Lord as a "man of prayer." Though He prayed often, Christ is only recorded as having prayed fifteen specific times in the Gospels. Luke records more of these occasions than any other writer – ten times in all. The Lord often sought the face of His Father early in the morning. Humanly speaking, the Lord was dependent upon His Father. He received instruction and strength from heaven.

Although the Lord Jesus spent much time in prayer, precious few details of His prayers are recorded. He presented a model prayer to His disciples in order to teach them how to pray; this was done at their request. He prayed before certain miracles, that the people might know of His Father in heaven. He prayed before eating, as shown in the "feeding of 5000," and at the "Last Supper."

What is really the "Lord's Prayer" is not what is vainly repeated in churches today, but what is recorded in John 17.

This is one of the longest prayers in the entire Bible, yet it only takes two or three minutes to read. In this tender petition of heaven, the Lord prays for Himself, His disciples, and all those who would believe after them. The Lord prayed for you and me (John 17:20-23).

## An Overview of the Life of Christ

Many books, some quite lengthy, have been written to expound various events of the Lord's life. The following overview serves to mark key events in the Life of Christ, as only Luke records them.

## Christ's Birth

*"No room in the inn"* pictures the condescending attitude of the world for Christ.

*"Wrapped in swaddling clothes"* depicts the clear purpose of His birth – to suffer and to die.

*"Laid in a manger"* declares the utter poverty of the Lord Jesus. Paul proclaims the result, *"that ye through His poverty might be rich" (2 Cor. 8:9).* The manger provided accessibility to all. If the Lord had been born in a palace, only the "well-to-do" and the nobility would have viewed Him. Yes, access to Him would have been limited in a palace but not so lying in the manger of a stable; any inquisitive soul who wanted to behold the Saviour was welcome, even lowly shepherds.

## Christ's Childhood

Only in Luke do we get a glimpse of Christ's childhood. The Lord is shown to us at the age of twelve in the temple: *"**sitting** in the midst of the teachers, both **hearing** them, and **asking** them questions."* Notice Luke's prevalent depiction of human exercise in the account.

Concerning the Lord's submission to parental authority, Luke informs us that *"He went down with them* [His parents], *and...was subject unto them" (Luke 2:51).* Until the Lord received new marching orders, He remained under the God-ordained authority He was placed under. This serves as a good example for all to follow. Godly authority is like a funnel, if we remain in proper relationship to it, God's blessings flow down to us through that funnel. If we rebel against it, we place ourselves under Satan's authority and lose the communion and blessings of God.

Christ experienced human growth and maturity: *"And Jesus increased in wisdom and stature and in favor with God and man" (Luke 2:52).* The Lord learned to eat, crawl, walk, talk, etc. in the same way you and I did. Perhaps the angels gasped when the Lord stumbled while learning to walk or wondered when He jabbered as a baby. How could we fully identify with Him in our human frailty if He did not experience all these things and more, as we do?

The Lord's home, until called to ministry, was Nazareth. Only Luke records that the Lord was "brought up" in Nazareth; Matthew merely states He returned there from Egypt.

## Christ's Ministry

Many wonderful details of Christ's ministry are highlighted only in Luke's Gospel. Here are but a few:

**Ministry begins.** Only Luke provides the age of the Lord when He entered His public ministry (Luke 3:23). He was about 30 years old, the same age in which a priest could sacrifice in the temple and a Jewish man could publicly read Scripture in the synagogue. The Lord did both, but the former was done outside the camp of Judaism (Heb. 13:12-14) at a place called Golgotha.

**Ministry at Nazareth.** Christ maintained every aspect of Jewish Law, including keeping the feasts of Jehovah and keeping the Sabbath day holy. It was His custom to visit the local synagogue on the Sabbath (Luke 4:16). Only Luke records the details of one particular Sabbath day in His hometown synagogue of Nazareth.

> *And He was handed the book of the prophet Isaiah. And when **He had opened the book, He found the place** where it was written: "The Spirit of the LORD is upon Me, Because He has anointed Me To preach the Gospel to the poor; He has sent Me to heal the brokenhearted, to proclaim liberty to the captives and recovery of sight to the blind, to set at liberty those who are oppressed; to proclaim the acceptable year of the Lord." Then He closed the book, and gave it back to the attendant and sat down. And the eyes of all who were in the synagogue were fixed on Him. And He began to say to them, "Today this Scripture is fulfilled in your hearing." Luke 4:17-21 (NKJV).*

Please notice that the Lord Jesus opened the book and then found the portion of Scripture to be read. The Holy Book did not just mystically open to the right location. The Lord expended effort to locate the portion of sacred text, just as you and I must turn pages in our Bibles. The Lord Jesus discontinued His reading of Isaiah's prophecy in the middle of a sentence to highlight His two advents to the earth. The remainder of Isaiah 61:1-2 reads, *"and the day of vengeance of our God; to comfort all that mourn."* In the incarnation, the Son of God had come to *"seek and to save,"* not to judge the wicked. His arm stretched forth to receive a nail, not to deliver a mortal blow from His sword. He came lowly and riding on the colt of an ass, not charging into battle upon His steed. When Christ was born, He brought God's offer of peace to the earth, as the angels declared on the night of His birth and He Himself declared to His disciples on resurrection day. Praise God that the Lord Jesus abruptly stopped when He did, or all humanity would have received the retribution of sin, God's wrath.

**Compassionate ministry.** Mark shows the busy ministry of the Lord, whereas Luke adds more detailed information concerning miracles to show Christ's compassionate side. The following three miracles serve as an example:

Only Luke records the resurrection of the widow of Nain's **only** son from the dead (Luke 7)

Only Luke states that Jairus' daughter, also raised from the dead, was his **only** daughter (Luke 8).

Only Luke mentions that the demon possessed boy, whom the Lord healed, was his father's **only** child (Luke 9).

It is evident from Luke's writings that the Lord feels the loss of children; He understands the home's need for children and was moved to compassionate service with each of these families.

**Forewarning ministry.** Only Luke affords the story of Lazarus and the rich man (Luke 16) to fully manifest the state of the lost after death. What Hebrews 9:27 states in a sentence, *"It is appointed unto men, once to die and after this the judgment,"* is vividly depicted with real life characters in this story. The Lord confirmed His love for those listening by solemnly warning them of the eternal reality of hell – *"the wages of sin is death."* The frank dialogue between Abraham and the rich man and the suffering imagery of the rich man's situation in hell should cause every unrepentant soul sleepless nights – for, as the rich man found out, that was his destiny.

**Friendly ministry.** It thoroughly provoked the pious Pharisees to anger, but the Lord often did it anyway – He "rubbed shoulders" with the "socially unacceptable." Only Luke refers to the Lord as *"a friend of publicans and sinners" (Luke 7:34)*. The Lord often talked with them about spiritual matters, sometimes in their homes while enjoying a meal and at other times during an impromptu meeting in the street. The Lord was available to anyone who was concerned about his or her soul. He spoke to the most vile – the demon possessed, the immoral, the distressed, and the brokenhearted – and met each one of their needs. The Lord did not have pagan-phobia. He loved all sinners and, at the same time, hated all their sin. Christ invested moments of time that the dead might live in eternity. How about you? Have you rubbed shoulders with any pagans lately?

# Christ's Suffering and Death

**The Garden of Gethsemane.** In comparing Luke and John's accounts of the events in the Garden of Gethsemane the night Christ was arrested, you might think the writers were speaking of two different instances. John describes a band of men approaching the Garden with *"lanterns and torches and weapons"* to seek out and arrest Jesus. Why were so many needed? Was Jesus a violent man? Was He leading a political rebellion? The answer to the latter questions is "No." In response to the first question, it is my opinion that the large number was to ensure that they would be able to search out and find a "hiding" Jesus on the Mount of Olives in the dark. Please keep in mind, it was the Pascal Feast and, thus, a full moon.

138

But, to their surprise, they did not have to search out a hiding Jesus:

> *Jesus therefore, knowing all things that would come upon Him, went forward and said to them, "Whom are you seeking?" They answered Him, "Jesus of Nazareth." Jesus said to them, "I am [He]." And Judas, who betrayed Him, also stood with them. Now when He said to them, "I am [He]," they drew back and fell to the ground. Then He asked them again, "Whom are you seeking?" And they said, "Jesus of Nazareth." Jesus answered, "I have told you that I am [He]. Therefore, if you seek Me, let these go their way," that the saying might be fulfilled which He spoke, "Of those whom You gave Me I have lost none"* (John 18:4-9, NKJV). Note: "He" in the above brackets is not within the Greek text.

In John, the Lord is shown to be the great I AM by referring to Himself by that name three times in response to the men before Him (The word "He" after "I am" is not in the Greek text.). Peter tried to kill a man, but the soldiers did not arrest Peter. Why? Because the Lord told them to let His disciples go, and that is just what they did. John declares once again that the Saviour is God in flesh, the Great I AM.

Luke equally declares the Lord's humanity. In Luke alone do we read of the Lord's anguish in prayer; *"His sweat was, as it were, great drops of blood falling" (Luke 22:44).* Only in Luke do we see angels ministering to Him in the garden. Luke is the sole Gospel writer to inform us that the Lord healed Malchus' ear after Peter severed it, and only Luke records that bewailing women were following the Lord and that He spoke to them.

Same event, but obviously recorded from two different perspectives to uphold the various glories of the Saviour.

**The crime superscription.** Both Luke and John document that the superscription hanging above the Lord's head at Calvary was in Greek, Latin, and Hebrew. As Luke is an appeal to humanity and John is writing to the whole world, it makes sense that the use of all three languages was recorded by these two evangelists. If Matthew had written concerning this detail, perhaps he would have only focused on the Hebrew language. Likewise, Mark would have likely referred to the language of the Roman Empire, Latin.

**Conversion of the dying thief.** Only Luke describes the Lord's conversations with the dying thief during the crucifixion account and then the thief's conversion prior to the Lord's death. The thief, quite familiar with suffering for wrongdoing, saw in the Lord's sufferings a purity and righteousness that both convicted him of his sinful state and caused him to look to the Saviour for salvation. How the words of the Saviour have encouraged and given hope to every saved sinner since: *"Today shalt thou be with Me in Paradise" (Luke 23:43)*. Paul would later declare this plainly, *"We are confident, I say, and willing rather to be absent from the body, and to be present with the Lord" (2 Cor. 5:8)*.

**Testimony of two lowly witnesses.** Pertaining to the Lord's civil trial, Matthew's two witnesses to the righteousness of Christ were figures of aristocratic influence (Pilate and his wife), but in Luke, the additional testimonies of two common folk are offered to declare the Lord's innocence. The repentant thief proclaimed, *"This Man hath done nothing amiss" (Luke 23:41)*. The Roman centurion declared, *"Certainly this was a righteous Man" (Luke 23:47)*. Even in such detail as this, the vantage points of Christ as **King** and **Man** are preserved between the Gospel accounts.

# Christ's Resurrection and Ascension

**Glorified humanity.** Only Luke acknowledges certain astonishing details of Christ's human behavior after His resurrection. Luke alone informs us of the long **walk** on the Emmaus Road while fellowshipping with two disciples. Only in the book of Luke do we read that the Lord **ate** food after His resurrection. Luke is the only Gospel to recount the Lord leading His disciples out of Jerusalem and to record that, before He departed to heaven, *"He lifted up His **Hands,** and blessed them"* *(Luke 24:50).*

**Carried up to heaven.** As mentioned previously, each Gospel writer concludes their account in a unique manner to climax their theme of Christ's glory. Matthew presents Christ in His kingdom on earth, while Mark records the ascension of Christ, then notes that He is still working with His disciples. Luke concludes his Gospel in no less a remarkable manner: *"It came to pass, while He blessed them, He was parted from them, and **carried up** into heaven"* *(Luke 24:51).* The Son of Man did not ascend back to heaven, but was **carried up** to heaven. The choice of words conveys a connotation of human frailty and the consequential necessity of God's helping hand.

Throughout his Gospel, Luke focuses his audience's attention to human events surrounding Christ's life, the humanity of the Lord Jesus, and the human appeal of His ministry. Luke presents a touchable Saviour who is more than willing to touch and bless others.

He wrestled with justice, that thou mightest have rest; He wept and mourned, that thou mightest laugh and rejoice; He was betrayed, that thou mightest go free; was apprehended, that thou mightest escape; He was condemned, that thou mightest be justified, and was killed, that thou mightest live;

He wore a crown of thorns, that thou mightest wear a crown of glory; and was nailed to the cross with His arms wide open, to show with what freeness all His merits shall be bestowed on the coming soul, and how heartily He will receive it into his bosom.[2]

– John Bunyan

# The Gospel of John

# "Behold Your God"

*O Zion, that bringest good tidings, get thee up into the high mountain; O Jerusalem, that bringest good tidings, lift up thy voice with strength; lift it up, be not afraid; say unto the cities of Judah,* **Behold your God!** *(Isa. 40:9).*

# Honor the Son

The Gospel of John is vastly different than the synoptic Gospels. The last of the four Gospels is the most exalted in tone and matchless in revealing the glorious splendor of Christ's deity. Is there any other portion of Scripture in which a man's hand was used to express such glorious anthems of Christ's divinity? In the first chapter alone, John introduces us to the eternally existing Word, His divine nature, and His distinct personage. Andrew Jukes comments on the dignified uniqueness of John's Gospel:

> Instead of the Lord of a kingdom, here it is "The Light of men." Instead of a Servant, here we see "Him who made all things." Instead of a Man subject to the powers of this world, born of a woman, laid in a manger, here it is "the Only-begotten Son, who is in the bosom of the Father," revealing His image, and communicating life "to as many as received Him" among the sons of men. Objections may be raised, and explanations offered, but the fact is beyond all doubt, that the views here [in John] rise, as the heaven is above the earth, over ... any which are given to us in the other Gospels.[1]

John is bestowed with the honor of presenting the Lord Jesus as the "Son of God." It is a divine title appearing more times in John than in any of the other Gospels. John does not introduce "a son of God," but *"the only begotten Son"* and *"the only begotten of the Father."* These expressions are found nowhere else in all of Scripture, save the one time John also declares this divine solidarity in his first epistle (1 Jn. 4:9). It was reserved for John to proclaim Jesus Christ as the unique Son of God to the whole world. In response the world should "honor the Son," an exhortation found six times in John's Gospel. In fact, of the twenty-two times the word "honor" is found in the four Gospels, thirteen reside in John. "Honor" is a key word pertaining to the fourth Gospel account. The Son of God is to be respected, revered and worshiped.

The special relationship of the Eternal Son of God with the Everlasting Father is exhibited in the Lord's frequent use of the expression "My Father." The phrase is found in John thirty-two times, compared to fifteen times in Matthew, not at all in Mark, and five in Luke. The Jews understood perfectly what the Lord was implying by the use of the term: *"Therefore the Jews sought the more to kill Him, because He not only had broken the sabbath, **but said also that God was His Father, making Himself equal with God"** (John 5:18).* The Jews sought to kill the Lord for a particular reason, one that He did not neglect to proclaim, and in fact restated again and again.

By using the expression "My Father," Christ was claiming a unique relationship with God that no one else possessed and enjoyed. It is ironic that the religious Jews of Christ's day perfectly understood the Lord's claim of deity, but the skeptics of our day allow their heads to swell with intellectual reasoning to avoid the clear facts of the matter. The discussion boils down to this: either Christ is who He said He was, the Son of God and the Saviour of the world, or He is the most notable liar that ever lived. The latter option is impossible, for the Lamb of God would not have been a sacrifice without blemish; consequently, we would still be dead in our trespasses and sin. There is absolutely no middle ground on this matter – Jesus Christ is

God incarnate. He claimed to be God and that was the blasphemous charge that the Sanhedrin determined He deserved death for (Mark 14:63-64; Luke 22:66-71). On this point, C. S. Lewis postulates:

> A man who was merely a man and said the sort of things Jesus said wouldn't be a great moral teacher. He'd be either a lunatic—on a level with a man who says he's a poached egg—or else he'd be the devil of hell. You must make your choice. Either this man was, and is, the Son of God, or else a madman or something worse.[2]

Matthew, Mark and Luke all demonstrate mankind's earthly connections with the Saviour. Matthew presented the Jewish claim upon Christ. Mark extends man's claim upon the Christ in service, while Luke shows Christ's identification with man in his lost state upon the earth. John's connection is much different than that of the synoptic Gospels. John relates Christ from a heavenly and spiritual point of view in connection with the believer. Might we ponder heaven's truth as we think upon the Lord Jesus Christ!

## The Author

The Gospel of John was written by the beloved disciple, who never refers to himself by name lest he distract from the divine person who is the subject of his writing. Matthew, a Jewish official (tax collector), was entrusted with presenting Christ's official glory as "King of the Jews." Mark, the humiliated servant, was chosen to write of Christ as the "Servant of Jehovah." Luke was privileged to address Christ's humanity. So why was John entrusted with the high honor of presenting Christ's deity?

I believe John wrote of the answer to this question:

*He that hath My commandments, and keepeth them, he it is that loveth Me: and he that loveth Me shall be loved of my Father, and **I will love him, and will manifest Myself to him** (John 14:21).*

Five times the night before the Lord was crucified, He told His disciples of the inseparable tie between their love for Him and practical obedience to His commands: *"If you love Me, keep my commandments" (John 14:15).* He was going to demonstrate this truth the next day: *"But that the world may know that I love the Father, and, as the Father gave Me commandment, even so I do" (John 14:31).* There was no question of the love of the Father for the Son, or of the Son for the Father, but the Son was going to show the world how much He loved the Father through obedience.

John 14:21 contains a promise for all those who will likewise demonstrate love for God by simply obeying His Word: The Lord said He would *"manifest Myself to him."* John was the beloved disciple and, apparently, the least inhibited in expressing his love for the Lord – it was to him, the disciple who loved much, that a fuller manifestation of Christ was granted. It was John, and only John, who was an eye witness to the Apocalypse, *"The Revelation of Jesus Christ" (Rev. 1:1).* The divine disclosure of Christ's glory to John is a direct testimony of the immensity of John's love for the Lord Jesus. Those who have been forgiven much love Christ more, those who love much obey Christ more, and those who obey Christ much comprehend Him more. May this be the aspiration of our heart, and no less, the thrill of life itself.

During Christ's ministry on earth, the seventy disciples were empowered and sent forth to preach throughout Israel (Luke 10). Then, there were the twelve disciples who received specialized ministry from the Lord. Then, there were the three: Peter, James and John. These three, and only these, were permitted to see the young maiden's resurrection, allowed to witness the Lord's transfiguration, and invited to pray with the Lord at Gethsemane. But then, there was the one: John, the beloved disciple, who, while reclining, laid his head on the Lord's breast. John was the only disciple that night to hear redeeming blood pump through the largest heart in the universe. Did the Lord forbid the other disciples from lying upon His breast? No. Their heart condition was what posed the constraint, not Christ. John's heart was unhindered, revealed, and open before the Lord; his urgency to express affection for the Lord could not be hindered.

Why was John entrusted with the care of the Lord's mother? Why was John assigned the momentous task of revealing majestic glory with pen upon paper? Because he loved much. The Lord has no favorites, but He does have intimates. There are many **professors** today who are quite content to follow the Saviour at a distance. They dare not venture nigh to the Lord for fear that His gentle and meek presence would condemn their shallow devotion. Dear believer, it requires a full and devout heart to venture as nigh to the Lord as John did that final disquieting night, but the blessing of knowing the Lord more deeply deems it a necessity. Abiding in Christ and continuing in His love is the only means of living a joyful and fruitful life. *"He that abideth in Me, and I in him, the same bringeth forth much fruit; for without Me ye can do nothing" (John 15:5). "If ye keep My commandments, ye shall abide in My love...that My joy might remain in you, and that your joy might be full" (John 15:10-11).*

## The Audience

Matthew's audience was Jewish; Mark wrote to the Romans, and Luke addressed the Greeks. Who is left? Anybody and everybody. John's audience is the whole world:

> *For God so loved the **world**, that He gave His only begotten Son, that whosoever believeth in Him should not perish, but have everlasting life. For God sent not His Son into the **world** to condemn the **world**; but that the **world** through Him might be saved (John 3:16-17).*

John refers to the world eighty times in his Gospel, compared to eighteen references in Matthew, five in Mark and ten in Luke. John has over twice as many references as the other three Gospels have combined. Unlike the synoptic Gospels, John uses the Roman reference of time in lieu of Jewish reckoning. This difference is important to understand; otherwise, there would appear to be serious disagreement between the Gospel writers on major events in the Lord's life. For example, Matthew states that, while Christ was on the cross, darkness covered the land at the sixth hour, but John records Christ was in the judgment hall before Pilate at the sixth hour. The sixth hour by Roman reckoning would be six o'clock, but the Jews would understand it to be twelve o'clock.

## Dispensational Content

Matthew and John contain the most dispensational content of the four Gospels. John announces the Jewish rejection by the eleventh verse of the first chapter. During the upper room discourse, the Lord told His disciples that He was leaving them to prepare a place for them in His Father's house and that He would likewise return for them (John 14:3). Israel's hope and inheritance is earthly, but the Church's is heavenly.

On another occasion, the Lord taught: *"Other sheep I have, which are not of this fold* [the Jewish fold.] *Them also I must bring, and they shall hear My voice; and there shall be one fold* [the Christian fold] *and one Shepherd" (John 10:16).* This wonderful truth was later expanded upon by Paul:

> *That at that time ye [Gentiles] were without Christ, being aliens from the commonwealth of Israel, and strangers from the covenants of promise, having no hope, and without God in the world: But now in Christ Jesus ye who sometimes were far off are made nigh by the blood of Christ. For He is our peace, who hath made both one, and hath broken down the middle wall of partition between us (Eph. 2:12-14).*

In the dispensation of the Church Age, *"There is neither Jew nor Greek, there is neither bond nor free, there is neither male nor female: for ye are all one in Christ Jesus" (Gal. 3:28).* Through the Lord's displayed love for the Church (the body of Christ composed of believing Jews and Gentiles), the nation of Israel will be made jealous and, in a future day, will turn back to Christ and be restored as God's covenant people (Rom. 11:11-14).

## The Uniqueness of John

John swells with unique content, planned omissions, key words, "types" of Christ, and declarations of deity. Here are a few examples of what makes John unique among the Gospels:

We obtain the full relation of the Holy Spirit's work concerning believers. He is the Comforter (literally, the advocate) of the believer. He is the Helper, the Teacher, the Convicter, and the Guide into deeper truth.

Christ is revealed as the "Word of God" and the "Bread from Heaven." Matthew presents Christ as fulfilling Old Testament prophecy, but John shows Christ as the literal fulfillment of Old Testament "types." The following serve as examples:

**The Lamb of God (John 1).** John the Baptist declared that Christ was *"the Lamb of God which taketh away the sin of the world" (John 1:29).* Paul agrees that Christ was the literal fulfillment of the Passover Lamb (Ex. 12): *"For even Christ our Passover is sacrificed for us" (1 Cor 5:7).* The millions of lambs slaughtered up until the time of Christ were a testimony that the blood of animals could never fully atone for man's sin; it was necessary for the perfect, unblemished, fully-tested Man, the Lamb of God, to shed His blood.

**The Serpent on the pole (John 3).** Jehovah brought fiery serpents among the people of Israel because of their murmuring and disbelief. Everyone bitten was ensured certain death unless, by faith, they looked upon a bronze serpent which Moses had hung on a high pole in the center of the camp (Num. 21). The uplook of faith was their only means to escape death. The serpent is symbolic of the spirit of sin and rebellion (Rev. 12:9) and the pole of the cross. Jesus declared, *"as Moses lifted up the serpent in the wilderness, even so must the Son of man be lifted up, that whosoever believeth in Him should not perish, but have eternal life" (John 3:14-15).* At Calvary, Christ became sin for us and took our place. Everyone who looks by faith to the Saviour's completed work on the cross shall not spiritually die but, rather, will live forever.

**The Well supplying living water (John 4).** The first occurrence of a **well** in the New Testament is when the Lord met a Samaritan woman with a devastated life at Jacob's well (John 4:6). He offered her "living water" (Himself) to satisfy her spiritually-parched soul. Interestingly, the first mention of a

**well** in the Old Testament is when the Lord met Hagar in the wilderness after she had fled the harsh treatment of her mistress Sarah (Gen. 16:7-14). How fitting for the all-sustaining Lord to meet a distressed woman fleeing for her life at a well in a desert place. Like Hagar, the Samaritan woman believed and obeyed the Lord and received a great blessing from Him. The prophet Isaiah writes, *"With joy shall ye draw water out of the wells of salvation" (Isa. 12:3).* A fountain of lasting joy springs up from the believer's spirit when Christ dwells within. For Hagar, this refreshment to her spirit was not found in Egypt (the world); it was received on the way to Shur (Gen. 16:7). How often the Lord has protected His children from entangling circumstances leading to despair, through direct communion with Himself on the way to Shur!

**The Manna from heaven (John 6).** John combines three "wilderness images" that the Lord used in his final months of ministry to speak of Himself as the only way of salvation: The manna from heaven (John 6), the water from a rock (John 7), and the pillar of fire at night (John 8). Specific Jewish rituals during the Feast of Tabernacles celebrated the latter two.

Seven times in John 6, the Lord Jesus refers to Himself as the "Bread of Life" which came down from heaven. He likens the Israelites feeding upon the manna in the wilderness in order to live, to a believer feeding upon Him now to obtain eternal life and to have the wherewithal to live for Him.

> *Moses gave you not that bread from heaven; but My Father giveth you the true bread from heaven. For the bread of God is He which cometh down from heaven, and giveth life unto the world....I Am the bread of Life; he that cometh to Me shall never hunger, and he that believeth on Me shall never thirst (John 6:32-35).*

153

Appropriating the finished work of Christ to one's account by faith is the only means of life, and applying His Word to our life in Him is the only means of living. His Word is our spiritual food!

**The Rock supplying living water (John 7).** The Lord often used Jewish traditions to speak of Himself. Edwin Blum and John Walvoord explain:

> The Feast of Tabernacles was celebrated with certain festival rituals. One was a solemn procession each day from the temple to the Gihon Spring. A priest filled a gold pitcher with water while the choir sang Isaiah 12:3. Then they returned to the altar and poured out the water. This ritual reminded them of the water from the rock during the wilderness wanderings (Num. 20:8-11; Ps. 78:15-16). It also spoke prophetically of the coming days of Messiah (Zech. 14:8, 16-19). The Feast's seventh and last day was its greatest (Lev. 23:36). Jesus stood, in contrast with the Rabbis' usual position of being seated while teaching. Said in a loud voice (John 1:15, 7:28; 12:44) was a way of introducing a solemn announcement. His offer, *Come to Me and drink*, was an offer of salvation (John 4:13, 6:53-56).[3]

**The Light of the World (John 8).** The Lord also used another occasion during the Feast of Tabernacles to publicly offer Himself as salvation. At this time, the Lord declared the second "I AM" statement recorded in John: *"I AM the light of the World; he that followeth Me shall not walk in darkness, but shall have the light of life" (John 8:12).* Warren Wiersbe explains:

> Our Lord's I AM statement was also related to the Feast of Tabernacles, during which a huge candelabra was lighted in

the temple at night to remind the people of the pillar of fire that had guided Israel in the wilderness journey.... To "follow" the Lord Jesus means to believe on Him, to trust Him; and the results are life and light for the believer.[4]

It is noted that the wicks of the lamps in the candelabra were made from the priest's worn-out garments. Hanging the lamps over the women's court at the temple ensured that **all** would be able to see the spectacular illumination. Christ utilized this traditional ceremony in a crucial spiritual sense to declare to the whole congregation, *"I AM the light of the world."* God's light, through Christ, was shinning forth to all mankind; its illumination had no prejudice to gender, ethnic origin, or social status. Christ came into the world and He died for the whole world (1 Jn. 2:2; Heb. 2:9), that *"whosoever will"* may step into the light and have fellowship with God (1 Jn. 1:5-9).

**The Good Shepherd (John 10).** The shepherd imagery of John 10 is actually only a portion of a New Testament trilogy. First, John presents Christ as the "Good Shepherd" who lays His life down for the sheep. Then the writer of Hebrews highlights the sanctifying work of the Lord Jesus as the Great Shepherd (Heb. 13:20-21). Finally, Peter proclaims Christ as the Chief Shepherd who will return and gather His sheep unto Him (1 Pet. 5:4), speaking of the return of Christ to the air to "snatch away" from the earth those who have truly believed on Him. May we contemplate the kindhearted words of our Lord:

*I am the Door: by Me if any man enter in, he shall be saved, and shall go in and out, and find pasture. The thief cometh not, but for to steal, and to kill, and to destroy: I am come that they might have life, and that they might have it more abundantly. I am the Good Shepherd: the good shepherd giveth His life for the sheep (John 10:9-11).*

His sacrificial love for the sheep stands in sharp contrast to the hireling shepherds of Israel, who led God's sheep astray, neglected their care, then deserted them in times of danger (Ezek. 34). Therefore, those who have been charged with the care of God's sheep must attend to His flock. Those, however, who would neglect this ministry should heed the Lord's decree against the base shepherds of Israel: *"I am against the shepherds and I will require my flock at their hand" (Ezek. 34:10).* Peter learned a valuable lesson after he had denied the Lord – it was easier to die for the Lord than to live for Him. Peter was later called to be one of many shepherds (elders) of God's sheep (1 Pet. 5:1-2), and although he could only be martyred once for the Lord, he would die a hundred times in caring for God's sheep. *"Simon, son of Jonas, lovest thou Me?...Feed my sheep" (John 21:16).* Let us heed the warning and selflessly tend to the Lord's own because we love the Lord.

**The Vine (John 15).** Some have made this passage (John 15:1-17) say what it does not – the analogy does not teach that true believers can lose their salvation. The subject matter is not salvation, but fruit bearing. Having just departed the upper room, the Lord is speaking only to His disciples (Judas had scurried off to work evil, leaving only true believers with the Lord.). The fact that Christ refers to "a man" and not "them" in verse 6 affirms that Christ knew the eleven were branches (true believers) in the Vine (in Him). The key words in this text are: "love" (ten occurrences), "abide" (nine times mentioned) and fruit (found eight times). The Lord's desire for every believer is that they abide in Him, experience the love and joy of God and yield spiritual fruit. Those who do not choose to abide in the goodness of Christ will be evident – there will be no spiritual fruit in their lives.

I will suggest two general applications from this passage. First, though some will give "lip service" as being branches in Christ, their mimicked fruit-bearing will be shown to be counterfeit spirituality in time. You can only fake it so long, without zapping yourself dry – Christ is the only true source of grace which produces spiritual fruit in believers (true branches in Him). True faith has a continuing reality (Jas. 2:17).

Secondly, the Greek word *airo*, translated "taketh away" in verse 2, is, in my opinion, better rendered as "lift up." This word has vast implications depending upon the context of the passage to which it is applied. In the New Testament, *airo* is rendered as some form of "taking away" twenty-two times and as some variation of "lifting up" thirty-six times. For example, Acts 4:24 reads, *"And when they heard that, they **lifted up** their voice to God with one accord."* So what does our kind and gentle Lord do when a believer (in Him) does not bear fruit? He cleans the sinful muck off them through the Word of God (John 15:3) and "lifts" them up in order to obtain better conditions for bearing fruit (John 15:2). The Lord does not, however, cast away every believer who in a moment of time becomes unfruitful because of sin. Note: It is the world that is ready and waiting to burn up a believer's testimony in verse 6 (It is not the Lord or angels, but men who gather and burn the fruitless branches.). This teaching addresses the **practice** of the believer and not his or her **position** in Christ. John holds up both the desire and the ministry of the Lord in John 15. He desires that all believers be fruitful by abiding in Him, and He also does His part as a loving caretaker to promote fruitfulness either by lifting and cleaning unfruitful branches or by pruning the already fruitful branches.

John Darby summarizes the passage:

> Christ, then was the true Vine; the Father, the Husbandman; the eleven were the branches. They were to abide in Him, which is realized by not thinking to produce any fruit except as in Him, looking to Him first. **Christ precedes fruit**. It is dependence, practical habitual nearness of heart to Him and trust in Him, being attached to Him through dependence on Him. In this way Christ in them would be a constant source of strength and of fruit. If, by abiding in Him, they had the strength of His presence, they should bear much fruit.[5]

# Key Words in John

John abounds with key words and phrases that distinctly highlight his theme of the Lord's deity. These would include: "Son of God," "My Father," "I AM," "world," "believe," "eternal life," "honor," "verily, verily," "love(d)," "light," and "life." There is a Christian camp in western New York called "Li-Lo-Li." The name is derived from three of the above key words found in John: Light, Love and Life. John stresses that when one believes in the light of God, they experience the love of God and receive eternal life. Note the distribution of these Gospel-related words among the four writers:

| Key Words | Matthew | Mark | Luke | John |
|---|---|---|---|---|
| Light | 14 | 1 | 13 | 24 |
| Love* | 13 | 7 | 15 | 57 |
| Life, Live* | 17 | 9 | 19 | 54 |
| Believe* | 10 | 17 | 11 | 99 |

The (*) denotes various forms of the word (i.e. loveth and loves).

Whereas Matthew stresses "righteousness" in association with the kingdom, John focuses on "eternal life." Both are connected and form one divine truth: Without life in Christ, one cannot display the righteousness of God. Why will the kingdom of God be full of righteousness? Righteousness is what emanates from the eternal God of the universe. All those who are born of God will radiate His righteous and holy life.

The words "repent" and "forgive" are not found in John because John conveys the Gospel message from a precise heavenly perspective. Spiritually speaking, the plain truth is shrouded in a sincere warning that is often introduced by the phrase "verily, verily." This phrase is not to be found in the other Gospels. One prevalent message in John is that in God is life, and apart from God is death. Man chose to be independent from God in the Garden of Eden and, consequently, brought death upon the entire race. In reality, the Lord Jesus was the first spiritually alive human to walk upon the planet since that dreadful day in which our first parents died. One cannot turn to Christ without repenting first (Luke 13:3, 5), but that is not John's emphasis. He speaks of death and life and of believing and not believing.

From the outset, John wants his audience to understand the basics of spiritual life and death. There is nothing like death to bring life into focus. *"All things were made by Him; and without Him was not any thing made that was made. In Him was life; and the life was the light of men" (John 1:3-4).* To Nicodemus, the inquisitive Pharisee, the Lord invited and warned: *"He that believeth on the Son hath everlasting life: and he that believeth not the Son shall not see life; but the wrath of God abideth on him" (John 3:36).* To beloved Martha, the Lord Jesus inquired, *"I am the resurrection, and the life: he that believeth in Me, though he were dead, yet shall he live. And whosoever liveth and believeth in Me shall never die.* **Believest thou this?** *" (John 11:25-26).*

## The Darkness of Disbelief

John 6 demonstrates that the unrighteous long to see a "sign or a wonder" in order to believe (John 6:30), while the righteous believe in order to see and understand (John 6:68-69). "Light," symbolizing divine truth, and "believing," an action of faith not based on sight, are paramount topics throughout John's Gospel. The anti-type of each of these is strongly tied together in the behavior of the spiritually blind Pharisees. They were blind because they chose to ignore the truth and continued in the darkness of self-righteousness.

> *And Jesus said, For judgment I am come into this world, that they which see not might see; and that they which see might be made blind. And some of the Pharisees which were with Him heard these words, and said unto Him, Are we blind also? Jesus said unto them, If ye were blind, ye should have no sin: but now ye say, We see; therefore your sin remaineth (John 9:39-41).*

Spiritual blindness clouds human reasoning, perverts logic and distorts our perception of reality. This is why, in spiritual matters, man must ignore sight-based faith, our mutable feelings, and simply trust God at His word – this is true faith. God rewards true faith by opening our understanding of spiritual truth; naturally speaking, we cannot understand the things of God (1 Cor. 2:9-13). *"Know the truth, and the truth shall make you free" (John 8:32).* Note the utter stupidity of the Pharisee's statements while speaking with the Lord Jesus:

These self-righteous strict law-keepers had to be reminded by Christ that their plans to murder Him were in fact breaking the Mosaic Law (John 7:19; 8:59)

Speaking to the Lord Jesus, the Pharisees said, *"Art thou also of Galilee? Search, and look; for out of Galilee ariseth no prophet" (John 7:52).* Perhaps, they had forgotten that Jonah was of Galilee.

The Pharisees brought a woman caught in the act of adultery before the Lord to be judged, but where was the man? The law condemned both to death; the law was no respecter of persons – such sin demanded the death of both parties (John 8:1-11; Lev. 20:10).

The Pharisees proclaimed to Christ that *"We be Abraham's seed, and were never in bondage to any man" (John 8:33).* But, in fact, they had been ruled by four world empires and had not been self-ruling for over 600 years.

Oswald Chambers once said, "Darkness is my point of view, my right to myself; light is God's point of view."[6] God has offered mankind a choice – to hide in the calamity of darkness and experience eternal death, or to abide in divine light and experience life in God. There can be no fellowship with God in darkness!

*This is the message which we have heard from Him and declare to you, that God is light and in Him is no darkness at all. If we say that we have fellowship with Him, and walk in darkness, we lie and do not practice the truth. But if we walk in the light as He is in the light, we have fellowship with one another, and the blood of Jesus Christ His Son cleanses us from all sin (1 Jn. 1:5-7, NKJV).*

## Omissions in John

**No parables in John.** Parables both revealed and concealed divine truth. For the seeker, the parable presented an opportunity to learn more, but for those who were rejecting Christ, the fuller truth would never be known (Matt. 13:10-13). The word parable is found thirty-two times in the Gospels, but only once in John. The Greek word rendered "parable" in John 10:6 is *paroimia*, literally meaning "a proverb" or a "figure of speech." J. H. Thayer defines it this way: "a saying out of the usual course or deviating from the usual manner of speaking,... any dark saying which shadows forth some didactic truth, especially a symbolic or figurative saying."[7] The normal Greek word used thirty-one times in the synoptic Gospels is *parabole*, meaning "a similitude implied by a fictitious narrative."[8] The Lord articulated the importance of Himself as the Good Shepherd in John 10, not an application-enriched story aimed at the listener.

**No genealogies**. In keeping with the priestly type of Christ presented in Melchizedek, the Lord is *"without descent, having neither beginning of days, nor end of life" (Heb. 7:3).* Because God is eternal, there simply is no genealogy that could establish *"The Ancient of Days."*

**No details of Christ's baptism.** From the synoptic Gospels we learn that John the Baptist did not want to baptize Christ, for he understood that he was unholy and that the Messiah needed no repentance. Christ, however, insisted that John baptize Him, for in His baptism Christ demonstrated His condescension to identify with those He came to save. John records none of these details, but does highlight God's own emblematic recognition of Christ as the Son of God. John the Baptist states the matter plainly shortly after Christ's baptism:

*And John bore witness, saying, "I saw the Spirit descending from heaven like a dove, and He remained upon Him. I did not know Him, but He who sent me to baptize with water said to me, 'Upon whom you see the Spirit descending, and remaining on Him, this is He who baptizes with the Holy Spirit.' And I have seen and testified that this is the Son of God. (John 1:32-34, NKJV).*

**No record of the temptation**. John presents Christ as God made flesh (John 1:14), and as James insists, *"God cannot be tempted" (Jas. 1:13).* This fact should put to death any degrading doctrines that pertain to the Lord's ability to sin or to His members having the capacity to be enticed to sin.

**No transfiguration.** This omission may seem puzzling, for didn't the transfiguration declare the inherent glory of Christ? Doesn't this fit John's theme? Yes, but where did the glory of Christ shine forth? On earth. John presents Christ from the heavenly view, not in an earthly relationship. Matthew gave prominence to Christ's kingly glory on earth; John speaks of the embedded glory that only heaven has witnessed and can fully comprehend. In the transfiguration, it is not the man who is God that is paramount, but that God became an earthly man. Samuel Ridout comments on the practical side of this truth:

> Our Lord is transfigured throughout the entire Gospel of John, but it is only to faith: *"We beheld his glory, the glory as of the Only Begotten of the Father."* No need for Him to manifest that glory visibly. His one great object throughout the Gospel is to bear witness to the truth of who He was and who had sent Him.[9]

**No appointed apostles**. In John, all ministry and work is designated for the hands of the Son of God (see John 2:23-25 as an example). In this way, Christ is ensured the preeminence among all those with whom He comes in contact. No sharing of ministry or glory is seen in John's Gospel, that would come after Christ's resurrection (John 17:22).

**No "prayers" by Jesus**. The most common Greek word associated with "praying" in the Gospels is *proseuchomai* (pros-yoo'-khom-ahee), which means "to pray to God either in supplication or worship." It is found forty-seven times in Matthew, Mark, and Luke but not once in John. The root word *proseuche,* also translated "prayer," occurs eight times in the synoptic Gospels but not at all in John. Another Greek word *deomai*, translated "beseech," "pray," "make request," is found nine times in the synoptic accounts, but again not in John. One more Greek word that is translated as "prayer," *erotao,* when added with the preceding three Greek words, accounts for nearly all references to prayer in the Gospels. *Erotao*, a verb that denotes "to ask from an equal," is translated "pray" or "prayed" only four times in Matthew, Mark and Luke and is used in reference to the realm of human speech (to show equality), not to the petitioning of the throne of heaven.

It is not hard for us to understand the application of the verb *erotao*. For example: If you and I were enjoying a meal together at our dining room table, I might ask you to "please pass the salt." I am speaking to you as an equal; it would be unbefitting for me to drop to my knees and petition you for the salt.

*Erotao* is associated with prayer seven times in John. Once it is used to illustrate the literal meaning "of asking:" *"Then they went out of the city, and came unto Him. In the mean while His disciples **prayed [asked]** Him, Master, eat. But He said unto them, I have meat to eat that ye know not of" (John 4:30-32).* This was clearly not a petition to God for something, but an expression of their concern for their leader. The remaining six occurrences are related to Christ "praying" to His Father or, literally, "talking to His Father as an equal." In all, *erotao* is translated "pray" seven times in John. Why is this significant?

The Lord Jesus explained the answer publicly, *"I and My Father are one" (John 10:30)*. The Jews clearly understood that He was asserting divine equality. Their response to the Lord's declaration is recorded in the next verse: *"Then the Jews took up stones **again** to stone Him" (John 10:31)*. Christ, being self-existing Himself, "spoke with" the Father as an equal not as a subordinate. John employs *erotao* to show the Lord's equality with His Father in normal speech. In essence, they are equal and speak as equals. In the other Gospels, the Lord prays to His Father as a subordinate, because as the Son of Man, He took on the form of a servant and, thus, lowered Himself in "position" not in essence.

**No "repent" or "forgive."** Matthew proclaims the earthly kingdom message of repentance and acceptance of the Messiah. Matthew, three times, applies the term "believe" in association with Christ's interaction with individuals. This term is never publicly proclaimed as part of the Gospel of the kingdom; repentance is stressed instead. John, however, stresses the heavenly perspective of mankind's spiritual condition and the ultimate solution – rebirth. In God is all life, and apart from God is death. John reckons all men spiritually dead and, thus, needing to be spiritually reborn (John 3:7) and quickened or made alive (John 5:21). It is necessary to repent to truly believe, but only by believing the Gospel can one be made alive.

**No apprehensions of the Cross.** As the "Son of God," Christ stood above His sorrow and grief, whereas the other Gospels record His apprehensions of the cross. What Luke records would be completely out of place in John: *"Father, if Thou be willing, remove this cup from Me,"* or *"being in an agony, He prayed more earnestly."* Not one word in John describes Christ's perspiration while praying in Gethsemane, but Luke writes, *"His sweat was, as it were, great drops of blood falling down to the ground."* These statements describe the *"Son* *of man"* as the *"man of sorrows."* John is the only one to present the heavenly view that night and, thus, highlights Christ's great expectation of being received into heaven, obtaining His glory again and being with His Father forevermore:

> *When Jesus knew that His hour was come that He **should depart out of this world unto the Father**, having loved His own which were in the world, He loved them unto the end (John 13:1).*

> *These words spake Jesus, and lifted up His eyes to heaven, and said, Father, the hour is come; **glorify Thy Son, that Thy Son also may glorify Thee** (John 17:1).*

> *I have glorified Thee on the earth: I have finished the work which Thou gavest Me to do. And now, O **Father, glorify Thou Me with Thine own self with the glory which I had with Thee before the world was** (John 17:4-5).*

**No ascension**. Each Gospel writer superbly concluded their account in a means which crescendoed their presentation of the Lord Jesus. In concluding his Gospel, John upholds the theme of the Lord's deity through the omission of the ascension of Christ to heaven. Why? Because the Son of God is omnipresent. The Lord avowed: *"And no man hath ascended up to heaven, but He that came down from heaven, **even the Son of man which is in heaven"** (John 3:13).*

John eloquently motivates every human soul to peer in and look beyond the veil of the Lord's flesh. In so doing, the Lord's divinity, lordship, moral splendor, and holy personage are appreciated and esteemed. Breathe it all in beloved; there is no sweeter refreshment to one's spirit, than to newly contemplate the glorious splendor of Christ.

# Holy, Holy, Holy

Just as Luke presents the life of Christ more uniquely than any other Gospel, John acclaims the deity of Christ like no other. Only God is perfect, self-sufficient, and self-existing – there is none like Him, for He is holy! *"For I am the Lord thy God, the **Holy One** of Israel, **Thy Saviour"** (Isa. 43:3). "I, even I, am the Lord, and **beside Me there is no Saviour"** (Isa. 43:11). "For I am God, and **there is none** else; I am God, and **there is none like Me"** (Isa. 46:9).* The prophet Isaiah clearly teaches that the Saviour of mankind is none other than the unique Holy God of the universe.

John uses plain language, Old Testament types and symbols, and numerical imagery to show that Jesus Christ is God in flesh – **holy humanity**. John expediently and emphatically introduces the Lord Jesus as being truly God, the Creator, in the opening verses of his account:

> *In the beginning was the Word, and the Word was with God, and **the Word was God**. The same was **in the beginning** with God. **All things were made by Him**; and without Him was not any thing made that was made. **In Him was life**; and the life was the light of men. And the light shineth in darkness; and the darkness comprehended it not (John 1:1-5).*

The Lord Jesus is holy! He was acknowledged as being holy in the womb by the angel Gabriel (Luke 1:35). Demons, while fearing premature judgment, asserted *"I know Thee who thou art, the Holy One of God" (Mark 1:24).* Peter proclaimed, *"We believe and are sure that thou art that Christ, the Son of the living God" (John 6:69).* Note: the Greek word *hagios* usually translated "holy" is connected with the word "Christ" in this passage. The early Church declared that Christ was holy (Acts 4:27, 30).

## The Sevens of John

The number seven is God's number throughout the Bible. Seven, as earlier stated, represents perfection and completeness; it is God's holy number. For this purpose, the number seven is employed at least sixteen times in John. The author humbly admits that there are likely more sevens which exist in John than what he is cognizant of presently.

**Seven** different people confess the Deity of Christ: John the Baptist, Nathanael, the Samaritan woman, Peter, the healed blind man, Martha, and Thomas.

**Seven** "I AM" titles are ascribed by Christ to Himself: "The Bread of Life," "The Light of the World," "The Door," "The Good Shepherd," "The Resurrection and the Life," "The Way, the Truth, and the Life," and "The True Vine."

**Seven** public miracles are recorded: He turned water to wine; He healed a nobleman's son who was near death; He healed the impotent man at the Pool of Bethesda; He fed 5000 men, plus women and children, from a boy's sack lunch; He calmed a raging storm while in the midst of it; He healed the man born blind, and He raised Lazarus from the dead.

**Seven** private manifestations of His deity: He knew Nathanael while he was still under the fig tree; He did not commit Himself to the people because He knew the thoughts of all men; He knew the sins of the Samaritan woman; He moved the disciples' boat instantaneously to Capernaum; He knew of

Lazarus' sickness and death without being told; He declared the details of Calvary to His disciples beforehand; and He provided a catch of 153 fish for His disciples.

**Seven** times *"These things have I spoken unto you"* appears in John.

**Seven** times Christ references His Father's "will."

**Seven** times Christ addressed the woman at the well (John 4).

**Seven** times Christ spoke of Himself as *"The Bread of Life" (John 6).*

**Seven** things the *"Good Shepherd"* does (John 10).

**Seven** times Christ made reference to *"the hour"* in which He would accomplish His Father's work.

**Seven** times Christ instructed His disciples to pray in His name.

**Seven** times the word "hate" is found in John 15.

**Seven** ministries of the Holy Spirit to the believer are noted (John 16).

**Seven** times Christ referred to believers as the Father's "gift" to Him (John 17).

**Seven** times John recorded that Christ spoke only the Word of the Father.

**Seven** times the writer of John (John) referred to himself but not by name.

**Seven** important events pertaining to Christ's ministry appear in all four Gospels: The ministry of John the Baptist as the forerunner of Christ, the feeding of the 5000, Peter's confession of Jesus being the Christ, the Triumphal Entry presentation of Messiah, and the crucifixion, burial and resurrection of the Lord.

## The Divine Attributes of Christ

Christ is Holy; the following are the divine attributes of Christ which John upholds to his audience:

**Creator:** *"All things were made by Him; and without Him was not anything made" (John 1:3).* Paul writes: *"For by Him were all things created, that are in heaven, and that are in earth, visible and invisible, whether they be thrones, or dominions, or principalities, or powers: all things were created by Him, and for Him: And He is before all things, and by Him all things consist" (Col. 1:16-17).* The Lord Jesus is the Creator and the Sustainer of all. He then must be Lord and Sovereign over all; thus, Paul refers to Him as the *"first born"* of creation to speak of His preeminence and authority over all things. He is not Michael the archangel, as some cults teach, or any created being for that matter, for how can one create themselves, be before themselves or maintain themselves – He created all things, and nothing was made without Him.

**Omnipresent:** John the Baptist spoke of the Lord Jesus, while He walked upon the earth: *"The only begotten Son, which is in the bosom of the Father" (John 1:18).* The Lord Himself declared, *"And no man hath ascended up to heaven, but He that came down from heaven, **even the Son of man which is in heaven**" (John 3:13).* Some Christians have a problem with the thought of the Lord being omnipresent and human. How can I see God in one place, and yet, He dwells everywhere? It is simply beyond human comprehension but not human observation. John wrote of the visible manifestation of all three persons of the Godhead in Revelation 4 and 5. He described the brilliant and majestic glory of the Father (Rev. 4:2-3) and then of the Father's hand (Rev. 5:1). He noted the representation of the Holy Spirit in seven fires before the throne of God (Rev. 4:5) and of the Lamb (the Lord Jesus) standing in the midst of the heavenly multitude (Rev. 5:6). All three persons of the Godhead are omnipresent but may choose to display their divine glory in just one particular location. The visible manifestation of Christ is fixed – glorified humanity forever. This attribute allows Christ to literally fulfill His promise to believers, *"I will never leave you nor forsake you"* (Heb. 13:5, NKJV).

**Omniscience:** The Lord said to Nathanael, *"Before that Philip called thee, when thou wast under the fig tree, **I saw thee"** (John 1:48).* Though many people sought Christ, most were half-hearted followers or just interested in a good story or seeing a supernatural wonder. Speaking of these, John writes, *"Jesus did not commit Himself unto them, because **He knew all men"** (John 2:24).* How astounded the Samaritian woman at the well must have been to hear the Lord's response to her denial of having a husband: *"Thou hast had five husbands; and he whom thou now hast is not thy husband"* (John 4:18). How is it possible for the Lord to know and to do anything that we ask in His name (John 14:14)? We understand that the asking is in accordance to His will (1 Jn. 5:14), but how is He to know our needs and hear our requests if He is not omniscient?

**Omnipotent:** The Lord, referring to Himself, said, *"Destroy this temple, and in three days I will raise it up"* (John 2:19). In Himself He had the power to lay down His life and raise it up again (John 10:17-18). He demonstrated His sovereign authority and power over creation by walking upon water, calming storms, feeding multitudes from a boy's sack lunch, moving a boat instantaneously across the sea of Galilee, and raising the dead. The demons feared His presence and yielded to His instruction (Luke 4:41; 8:28). Satan was rebuked by Christ and submitted to His command (Matt. 4:10-11).

**Equality with the Father:** *"I and my Father are one" (John 10:30).* Again, the Jews understood perfectly the Lord's claim: *"Therefore the Jews sought the more to kill him, because He not only had broken the Sabbath, but said also that God was His Father, making Himself equal with God" (John 5:18).* Albert Barnes comments to the vast weight of the Lord's statement – His affirmation of deity:

> The word translated "one" is not in the *masculine*, but in the *neuter* gender. It expresses *union*, but not the precise nature of the union. It may express any union, and the particular kind intended is to be inferred from the connection. In the previous verse He had said that He and His Father were united in the same object – that is, in redeeming and preserving His people. It was this that gave occasion for this remark. Most of the Christian fathers understood [this verse] … as referring to the oneness or unity of nature between the Father and the Son; and that this was the design of Christ appears probable from the following considerations: **First.** The question in debate was not about His being united with the Father in plan and counsel, but in power. He affirmed that he was able to rescue and keep His people from all enemies, or that He had power superior to men and devils – that is, that He had supreme power over all creation. He affirmed the same of His Father. In this, therefore, they were united. **Second.** The Jews understood Him as affirming His equality with God, for they took up stones to punish Him for blasphemy (John 10:31, 33), and they said to Him that they understood Him as affirming that He was God. **Third.** Jesus did not deny that it was His intention to be so understood. **Fourth.** He immediately made another declaration implying the same thing, leaving the same impression, and which they attempted to punish in the same manner (John 10:37-39). If Jesus had not intended so to be understood, it cannot be easily reconciled with moral honesty that He did not distinctly disavow that such was His intention. The Jews were

well acquainted with their own language. They understood Him in this manner, and He left this impression on their minds.[1]

**Eternal:** *"In the beginning was the Word and the Word was with God and the Word was God. The same* [the Word] *was **in the beginning** with God" (John 1:1-2). "**Before** Abraham was I Am" (John 8:58).* The fact that He created all things is solid evidence that He is God, the pre-existent One (John 1:3-4). *"And now, O Father, glorify thou Me with Thine own self with the glory which I had with Thee before the world was" (John 17:5).* The Lord Jesus is the eternal Son of God, the *"Alpha and Omega, the first and the last" (Rev. 1:11).*

**True:** *"I am the Way, **the Truth**, and the Life, no man cometh unto the Father, but by Me" (John 14:6).* There is no other way to enjoy eternal paradise with God than through the person of Jesus Christ. Thomas A Kempis wrote of the Lord Jesus: "I am the Way unchangeable; the Truth infallible; the Life everlasting."[2] His blood alone washes away sin, and only through His sacrifice can a repentant, believing sinner be justified – receive a righteous standing before God.

**Just:** *"My judgment is **just**" (John 5:30). "For the Father judgeth no man, but hath committed all judgment unto the Son" (John 5:22).* Speaking of the just Judge, Paul declares: *"For it is written, As I live, saith the Lord, every knee shall bow to Me, and every tongue shall confess to God. So then every one of us shall give account of himself to God" (Rom. 14:11-12). "Wherefore God also hath highly exalted Him, and given Him a name which is above every name. That at the name of Jesus every knee should bow, of things in heaven, and things in earth, and things under the earth" (Phil. 2:9-10).*

**Holy and Sinless:** When the Lord Jesus asked, *"Which of you convicts Me of sin?" (John 8:46, NKJV),* no one said a word! Albert Barnes comments to the significance of the Lord's question:

> The word sin here evidently means error, falsehood, or imposture. It stands opposed to truth. The argument of the Saviour is this: A doctrine might be rejected if it could be proved that he that delivered it was an impostor; but as you cannot prove this of me, you are bound to receive my words.[3]

**Love:** *"**Greater love hath no man** than this, that a man lay down his life for his friends" (John 15:13).* The Lord is love, displayed sacrificial love for others and exhorted His disciples to do the same:

> *Beloved, let us love one another: for love is of God; and every one that loveth is born of God, and knoweth God. He that loveth not knoweth not God; for God is love. In this was manifested the love of God toward us, because that God sent His only begotten Son into the world, that we might live through him. Herein is love, not that we loved God, but that he loved us, and sent his Son to be the propitiation for our sins (1 Jn. 4:7-10).*

**Grace:** *"We beheld His glory, the glory as of the only begotten of the Father, **full of grace** and truth (John 1:14).* The Lord's example should be followed by all those who name Him as Saviour – let us not be just balanced, but full of grace and truth. The Apostle Paul puts it this way: *"Let your speech be always with grace, seasoned with salt" (Col. 4:6).* If it was not necessary to say, or if it could not be said in love, or if it were not true, the Lord Jesus did not say it.

**Unique Son of God:** Concerning Christ, God the Father revealed to John the Baptist, *"This is the **Son of God**" (John 1:34),* and *"The only begotten of the Father" (John 1:14).* The Lord affirmed: *"He that hath seen Me, hath seen the Father" (John 14:9).* Only the Lord has such a special relationship with the Eternal Father as evidenced by the frequent use of the phrase *"My Father."* As mentioned earlier, the phrase is found in John thirty-two times. The Jews understood perfectly what the Lord was implying by the use of the term: *"Therefore the Jews sought the more to kill Him, because He not only had broken the Sabbath, but said also that God was His Father, making Himself equal with God" (John 5:18).* The Jews sought to kill the Lord for one particular reason; a reason He did not neglect in proclaiming but, conversely, restated again and again – He was the unique eternal Son of God.

**Laid Aside His Glory:** While speaking to His Father, the Lord Jesus said: *"I have glorified thee on the earth: I have finished the work which thou gavest me to do. And now, O Father, glorify thou me with thine own self with the glory which I had with thee before the world was" (John 17:4-5).* The Apostle Paul explains precisely what the Son of God did to effect propitiation for human sin:

> *Let this mind be in you which was also in Christ Jesus, who, being in the form of God, did not consider it robbery to be equal with God, but made Himself of no reputation, taking the form of a bondservant, and coming in the likeness of men. And being found in appearance as a man, He humbled Himself and became obedient to the point of death, even the death of the cross. Therefore God also has highly exalted Him and given Him the name which is above every name, that at the name of Jesus every knee should bow, of those in heaven, and of those on earth, and of those under the earth,*

*and that every tongue should confess that Jesus Christ is Lord, to the glory of God the Father (Phil. 2:5-11, NKJV).*

The Lord's utter humility and sacrificial behavior in serving others is an example for all to follow. To the extent that He was despised and disgraced by mankind, God has highly exalted Him above all power and principalities, to be esteemed, worshipped and appreciated.

**Controls Time and Events:** *"They sought to take Him: but no man laid hands on Him, because His hour was not yet come" (John 7:30).* In the Garden of Gethsemane, the Lord commanded the very soldiers that were arresting Him to take only Him and let His disciples go – this after Peter tried to kill a man (John 18:8-12). And let us remember the divine dignity of our Lord's words, *"No man taketh it* [speaking of His life] *from Me, but I lay it down of myself. I have power to lay it down and I have power to take it up again" (John 10:18).*

**The Light of the World:** *"Then spake Jesus again unto them, saying, I am the light of the world: he that followeth Me shall not walk in darkness, but shall have the light of life" (John 8:12).* He was the Light of heaven for all men to witness real and eternal life. *"In him was life; and the life was the light of men. And the light shineth in darkness; and the darkness comprehended it not" (John 1:4-5).* Concerning this truth, Andrew Jukes notes:

> There stood One, in a servant's form, in the likeness of sinful flesh, whose life, even while others judged Him, was judging everything, and showing, by its holy contrast, what was in men and what was not, according to God's mind. "The Life was the Light."[4]

176

The first Adam was originally created in the "likeness" and "image" of God, but, after the fall, moral "likeness" was lost, and man would bear God's "image" with diminished capacity. Man was still God's representative on earth, but not a very good one. Genesis 5:3 states that Adam begot children *"in his own likeness, after his image."* Image is not likeness; these are distinctly different ideas. Likeness is similitude, being like; image is representation, whether alike or not. The Lord Jesus, *the last Adam,* is never spoken of as "being in the likeness of God." He cannot be "like" God since He is God. Adam's descendants, though still representing God, would be like their father Adam in moral likeness. The Lord Jesus Christ, being fully God, revealed the glory of God on earth as only a Holy God could. Though the first Adam failed to represent God and show forth God's moral glory, the last Adam achieved perfect representation. *"And the Word was made flesh, and dwelt among us, (and we beheld His glory, **the glory as of the only begotten of the Father**,) full of grace and truth (John 1:14).*

# The Aspiration

# of the Gospels

# Behold the Saviour

In the beginning of our study together, we contemplated the four unique **"behold"** statements found within the Old Testament. These prepare the way for Christ's first earthly advent, and each one emphasizes a distinct Gospel theme. As previously stated, each **"behold"** declaration is a unique invitation by God the Father for all humanity to gaze upon and admire His dear Son.

> *Behold your King (Zech. 9:9)* – Gospel of Matthew
> *Behold My Servant (Isa. 42:1)* – Gospel of Mark
> *Behold the Man (Zech. 6:12)* – Gospel of Luke
> *Behold your God (Isa. 40:9)* – Gospel of John

What is additionally fascinating is that the same Old Testament declarations which prepared the way for the Lord's incarnation are repeated in the New Testament as explicit confirmation that Jesus Christ was the direct fulfillment of these Old Testament proclamations:

> **Behold My Servant**, *whom I have chosen; My beloved, in whom My soul is well pleased: I will put My spirit upon Him, and He shall show judgment to the Gentiles (Matt. 12:18).*

*Then came Jesus forth, wearing the crown of thorns, and the purple robe. And Pilate saith unto them,* **Behold the Man** *(John 19:5)!*

*And it was the preparation of the passover, and about the sixth hour: and he saith unto the Jews,* **Behold your King** *(John 19:14)!*

**Behold***, a virgin shall be with child, and shall bring forth a son, and they shall call His name Emmanuel, which being interpreted is,* **God with us** *(Matt. 1:23)* – literally *"Behold your God!"*

The New Testament authentication of Christ is completely homogeneous with the pronoun coupling found in the Old Testament announcements. As explained earlier, when the Lord is presented in a position of authority (as King and as God), the possessive pronoun "your" precedes the title, but when the position of a lowly servant is stated, the pronoun "My" appears. When the Lord is introduced in the intermediate stature, as a man, the neutral "the" is applied. This arrangement demonstrates the various facets and positional glories of the Lord's ministry and how He would relate to mankind.

The whole of the Bible speaks of Christ; He is God's personal message and invitation to mankind! He is the spirit of prophecy (Rev. 19:10); all promises of God are yea in Him (2 Cor. 1:20). The believer's complete identity and existence abides with and in Christ. He is our peace (Eph. 2:14), our joy (John 15:11), and our hope (Tit. 2:13). He is the foundational Stone of our faith (1 Cor. 3:11), the Shepherd and Bishop of our souls (1 Pet. 2:25), the Head of the Church (Col. 1:18), our Great High Priest (Heb. 4:15), our Advocate with the Father (1 Jn. 2:1), and our Saviour (Eph. 5:23). He is Lord of lords and King of kings (1 Tim. 6:15), the Judge of all (Matt. 25:31-33), the Alpha and the Omega (Rev.

1:11), the Creator (Col. 1:16-17) and the only begotten Son of God (John 3:16). Without Christ, there is no salvation, no life, and no hope!

> *For by Him were all things created, that are in heaven, and that are in earth, visible and invisible, whether they be thrones, or dominions, or principalities, or powers: all things were created by Him, and for Him: And He is before all things, and by Him all things consist. And He is the head of the body, the church: who is the beginning, the firstborn from the dead; **that in all things He might have the preeminence** (Col 1:16-18).*

Understanding who Christ is and what the believer has in Christ should compel every true Christian to reach *"forth unto those things which are before"* and to *"press toward ... the high calling of God in Christ Jesus"* (Phil. 3:13-14).

Why does God bless the believer? Because the Father loves His Son, and we, being *"in Christ,"* will then be the object of God's love and blessing. These blessings in Christ can be identified by scanning Scripture for such phrases as *"in Christ,"* *"in Jesus Christ,"* or *"in Christ Jesus."* These expressions are not found in the Gospel accounts and are only found once in the book of Acts. However, the Epistles, which unveil the manifold wisdom and mysteries of God concerning Christ's accomplishments, have over eighty references to these phrases. It is noted that the phrase *"with Christ"* speaks of positional or identification truths, while the phrase *"in Christ"* normally speaks of blessing resulting from our spiritual union with the Son of God.

What do we have *"in Christ"*? We have...
- Redemption (Rom. 3:24)
- No condemnation (Rom. 8:1)
- Spirit of life (power over sin) (Rom. 8:2)

183

- The love of God (Rom. 8:39)
- Oneness in the body of Christ (Rom. 12:5)
- Sanctification (1 Cor. 1:2)
- Hope (1 Cor. 15:19)
- Life (1 Cor. 15:22)
- Triumph, by God's grace (2 Cor. 2:14)
- Been made a new creation (2 Cor. 5:17)
- Liberty (Gal. 2:4)
- Been made children of God (Gal. 3:26)
- Equality (Gal. 3:28)
- All spiritual blessings in heavenly places (Eph. 1:3)
- Been created unto good works (Eph. 2:10)
- Salvation (2 Tim. 2:10)
- Preservation (Jude 1)

As the believer maintains an impassioned focus on the Lord and recalls to mind all that we have *"in Him,"* life's circumstances do not seem so overwhelming. What we have spiritually in Christ is not comparable with the cheap and temporary trinkets we clutch presently. Charles H. Spurgeon rightly expressed the spiritual reality of every human soul: "I have a great need for Christ; I have a great Christ for my need."[1] Just before dying in 1770, George Whitefield declared: "How willing I would ever live to preach Christ! But I die to be with Him!"[2] These great men of faith, despite opposition and hardship, were obsessed with Christ. Their passion for Christ, and that of others, ignited an evangelical blaze which swept across two continents and saw thousands of souls won to Christ. Their lives counted for eternity because they counted Christ worthy.

# Jesus Wonderful Lord

Born among cattle in poverty sore,
Living in meekness by Galilee's shore,
Dying in shame as the wicked ones swore,
Jesus, wonderful Lord.

Weary oft – He is the world's only rest;
Hungry and thirsty – with plenty has blest;
Tempted – He promises grace for each test;
Jesus, wonderful Lord.

Friend of the friendless – betrayed and denied,
Help of the weak – in Gethsemane cried,
Light of the world – in gross darkness He died,
Jesus wonderful Lord.

– Paul White

# What is the Aspiration of the Gospels?

We have briefly viewed the unfathomable mind of God in the Gospels. The literary design, the theme development, the different writing styles, the diverse human agents, the omissions, the inclusions, the variations, the key words and phrases, the embellished details, and much more speak of one Supreme Mind. May we praise God for both His effort in portraying His Son to us in such a unique fashion and for the One in whom all Scripture centers – The Lord Jesus Christ.

What is the main aspiration of the Gospel message? John affords a vital summary: *"And many other signs truly did Jesus in the presence of His disciples, which are not written in this book: But these are written, that ye might **believe that Jesus is the Christ,** the Son of God; and **that believing ye might have life** through His name" (John 20:30-31).* Did you notice the two "believes" in this passage? In the Greek language, the first "believe" is in the "aorist" tense, while the second is in the "present" tense. John wrote his record of Christ for two reasons. First, that we might believe, speaking of a unique action in the past, which has a continuing effect – this relates to trusting the Gospel message for salvation and being regenerated. After receiving eternal life, the second "believe" becomes most important. This believing should be continuous and progressing in maturity such that the believer displays and enjoys the life of Christ more and more and, no less, learns to love the Lord more and more.

Many Christians today, like the second generation of Christians at Ephesus, are retaining doctrinal purity, maintaining a blameless life, and serving the Church continuously, yet they lack a deep devotion to Christ. The Church today must heed the same warning that Christ issued to them:

> *Nevertheless I have somewhat against thee, because thou hast left thy first love. Remember therefore from whence thou art fallen, and repent, and do the first works; or else I will come unto thee quickly, and will remove thy candlestick out of his place, except thou repent (Rev. 2:4-5).*

The Lord doesn't want just followers; He wants disciples that will die to self and live for Him. Orthodoxy and ministry are not enough; Christ demands the believer's heart, as well as his or her hands and head. Those believers who deny Him as their first love will ultimately lose their testimony for Christ. Our love for experiencing His life, what an exchange!

Our desire to be a disciple of Christ is a direct measure of how much we truly love Christ and believe His message. The reason we hold back from being fools for Christ, and thus, from seeing the mighty hand of God in our lives, is disbelief – we don't trust God. Through disbelief, the One who was offended for us becomes an offense to us. Oswald Chambers precisely identified the problem: "Jesus Christ always speaks from the source of things; consequently those who deal only with the surface find Him an offense."[1] The Lord Jesus didn't teach a middle ground concerning discipleship; consequently, it is all or nothing:

*If any man come to Me, and hate not his father, and mother, and wife, and children, and brethren, and sisters, yea, and his own life also, he cannot be My disciple (Luke 14:26).*

*And whosoever doth not bear his cross, and come after Me, cannot be My disciple (Luke 14:27).*

*So likewise, whosoever he be of you that forsaketh not all that he hath, he cannot be My disciple (Luke 14:33).*

*And why call ye Me, Lord, Lord, and do not the things which I say? (Luke 6:46).*

Don't call Christ, Lord, if you are not doing what He commands. He must be Lord of all, or He is not Lord at all. Christianity is more than coming to the Lord for salvation; it is also going on with Him in spiritual life. The Gospel message pleads for the hell-bound sinner to embrace the cross of Christ, and no less so for the heaven-bound saint to take up his or her cross that he or she might enjoy life now. The Lord does not want us to only believe upon Him to evade judgment; He wants us to become like Him through progressive and continuous believing. If we truly believe the Gospel message, we will yield to Him and experience His life now.

*I am the door: by Me if any man enter in, he shall be saved, and shall go in and out, and find pasture. The thief cometh not, but for to steal, and to kill, and to destroy: **I am come that they might have life, and that they might have it more abundantly** (John 10:9-10).*

Dear reader, do you truly believe the complete Gospel message of Jesus Christ? Are you presently experiencing the fullness of Christ's life – His abiding love, infusing power, immense joy, and tranquilizing peace? If not, repent, believe, and yield – you will never regret experiencing heaven before getting there. Through His Gospel, Christ offers both eternal and abundant life – this is the aspiration of the Gospel message. So, determine to live – live for Christ now and experience the full abundant life that only He can offer! A. W. Tozer once exhorted: "The whole course of the life is upset by failure to put God where He belongs."[1]

Concerning the abundant life in Christ, a young John Wesley once wrote, "O Lord, let me not live to be useless." God answered that humble prayer. Wesley traveled tens of thousands of miles on horseback to preach the Gospel of Jesus Christ to whoever would listen. He witnessed thousands of souls trust Christ for salvation. In the autumn years of his life Wesley wrote:

> Today I entered on my eighty-second year and found myself just as strong to labor and as fit for any exercise of body or mind as I was forty years ago. I do not impute this to second causes, but to the Sovereign Lord of all. It is He who bids the sun of life stand still, so long as it pleases Him. I am as strong at eighty-one as I was at twenty-one; but abundantly more healthy, being a stranger to the headache, toothache, and other bodily disorders that attended me in my youth. We can only say, "The Lord reigneth!" **While we live, let us live to Him!**[2]

The night before His crucifixion the Lord Jesus earnestly requested of His Father *"that they also whom thou hast given Me, be with Me where I am; that they may **behold My glory"** (John 17:24).* Dear believer, if you are not living the abundant life of Christ, lift your eyes afresh to heaven, and **behold the Saviour**. Our life is hidden in Christ, and you cannot love selflessly if you love not Him; and you cannot live abundantly if you live not Him!

> All for Jesus, all for Jesus!
> All my being's ransomed powers:
> All my thoughts and words and doings,
> All my days and all my hours.
> Let my hands perform His bidding,
> Let my feet run in His ways;
> Let my eyes see Jesus only,
> Let my lips speak forth His praise.

– Mary D. James

# Endnotes

## The Gospel Accounts

1. William MacDonald, *Believer's Bible Commentary* (Thomas Nelson Publishers, Nashville, TN; 1989), p. 1197
2. Samuel Ridout, *The Serious Christian* (Books for Christians, Charlotte, NC; no date), p. 12
3. C. I. Scofield, *The New Scofield Study Bible* (Oxford University Press, New York; 1967), p. 987
4. Samuel Ridout, op. cit., p. 24.
5. A. T. Robertson, *A Harmony of the Gospels* (Harper & Row Publishers, New York, NY; 1922), Preface
6. J. G. Bellett, *The Evangelists, Meditations on the Four Gospels* (Bible Truth Publishers, Addison, IL; no date), Introduction
7. F. W. Grant, *The Numerical Structure of Scripture* (Loizeaux Brothers, Bible Truth Depot, New York, NY; 7th printing 1956), pp. 122-123
8. William Kelly, *Introductory Lectures NT Vol. The Gospels* (Believers Book Shelf, Sunbury PA; 1970 reprint), pp. 143-144
9. Andrew Jukes, *Four Views of Christ* (Kregel Publications, Grand Rapids, MI; 1966), p. 15
10. J. G. Bellett, op. cit., p. 4

## Why Four Gospels?

1. J. F. Walvoord, R. B. Zuck, & Dallas Theological Seminary, *The Bible Knowledge Commentary : An Exposition of the Scriptures* (Victor Books, Wheaton, IL; 1983-1985), p. 172

## Why Four Gospel? (cont.)

2.  Ibid., p. 172
3.  F. W. Grant, *Genesis – In the Light, The Serious Christian Series* (Loizeaux Brothers, Inc., Neptune, NJ), pp. 6-7
4.  F. W. Grant, *The Numerical Structure of Scripture*, op. cit. p. 42
5.  William MacDonald, op. cit., p. 1198

## Why is Matthew First?

1.  Edythe Draper, *Draper's Quotations from the Christian World* (Tyndale House Publishers Inc., Wheaton, IL – electronic copy)

## The Nobility of Matthew

1.  L. Laurenson, *Classic Christian Commentary* (Books for Christians, Charlotte, NC; no date) p. 60
2.  C. I. Scofield, op. cit., p. 994, note 3
3.  William MacDonald, *Here's the Difference* (GOSPEL FOLIO PRESS, Port Colborne, ON; 1999), pp. 119-120
4.  L. Laurenson, op. cit., p. 44
5.  Arthur Pink, *Why Four Gospels?* (Scripture Truth Book Co., Fincastle, VA; no date), pp. 109-110
6.  Ibid., pp. 46-47
7.  Edythe Draper, op. cit.
8.  William MacDonald, *Believer's Bible Commentary*, op. cit., p. 1215
9.  Arthur Pink, op. cit., pp. 45-46

## A Serving Saviour

1.  Andrew Jukes, op. cit., p. 56
2.  Hamilton Smith, *Classic Christian Commentary – Matthew* (Books for Christians, Charlotte, NC; no date), pp. 1-3
3.  Edythe Draper, op. cit.
4.  Arthur Pink, op. cit., p. 75
5.  Dr. Howard Taylor, *Spiritual Secret of Hudson Taylor* (Whitaker House, New Kensington, PA; 1996), p. 368

## A Serving Saviour (cont.)

6. Warren Wiersbe, *The Bible Exposition Commentary, Vol. 1* (Victor Books, Wheaton, IL; 1989), p. 416
7. William MacDonald, *Here's the Difference*, op. cit., p. 186

## God was Manifest in Flesh

1. Andrew Jukes, op. cit., p. 21
2. William Kelly, op. cit., p. 143
3. David Gooding, *According to Luke* (GOSPEL FOLIO PRESS, Port Colborne, ON; 1987), p.9
4. J. N. Darby, *Synopsis of Books of the Bible Vol. 5* (Stow Hill Bible and Tract Depot, Kingston, ON; 1949), p. 202
5. Ibid., p. 183
6. Edythe Draper, op. cit.
7. William G. Moorehead, *The Fundamentals of Christianity: The Moral Glory of Jesus Christ* (Biblesoft, Electronic Database, 1997)
8. J. N. Darby, *The Holy Scriptures: A New Translation from the Original Languages* (Logos Research Systems, Oak Harbor; 1996), electronic copy – 1 Timothy 3:16
9. Edythe Draper, op. cit.
10. Edythe Draper, op. cit.
11. J. N. Darby, *The Holy Scriptures,* op. cit., Hebrews 4:15
12. William Newell, *Hebrews Verse by Verse* (Moody Press, Chicago, IL; 1947), p. 148
13. H. A. Ironside, *Hebrews* (American Bible Conference; Philadelphia, PA; 1932), p. 67
14. J. N. Darby, *Synopsis of Books of the Bible Vol. 5,* op. cit., p. 179
15. F. W. Bruce, *The Serious Christian, Notes on Hebrews* (Books for Christians, Charlotte, NC; no date), p. 26
16. William Kelly, *The Serious Christian, Hebrews* (Books for Christians, Charlotte, NC; no date), p. 49
17. Andrew Jukes, op. cit., p. 71

## The Life of Christ

1. Arthur Pink, op. cit., pp. 162-163

## The Life of Christ (Cont.)

2. Edythe Draper, op. cit.

## Honor the Son

1. Andrew Jukes, op. cit., pp. 92-93
2. Edythe Draper, op. cit.
3. John Walvoord, *The Bible Knowledge Commentary* (Victor Books, Wheaton, IL; 1985), p. 301
4. Warren Wiersbe, op. cit., p. 320
5. J. N. Darby, *Synopsis of Books of the Bible Vol. 3,* op. cit., p. 375
6. Edythe Draper, op. cit.
7. J. H. Thayer, *Thayer's Greek Lexicon* (Biblesoft; 2000), electronic database
8. James Strong, *New Exhaustive Strong's Numbers and Concordance with Expanded Greek-Hebrew Dictionary* (Biblesoft and International Bible Translators, Inc.; 1994), electronic copy
9. Samuel Ridout, op. cit., p. 171

## Holy, Holy, Holy

1. Albert Barnes, *Barnes' Notes – The Gospels* (Baker Book House, Grand Rapids, MI; 1884 reprint), p. 293
2. Edythe Draper, op. cit.
3. Albert Barnes, op. cit., pp. 273-274
4. Andrew Jukes, op. cit., p. 107

## Behold the Saviour

1. Edythe Draper, op. cit.
2. John Pollock, *George Whitefield and the Great Awakening* (Doubleday and Co., Garden City, NY; 1972), p. 19

## What is the Aspiration of the Gospels?

1. Edythe Draper, op. cit.
2. Ibid.

# Bibliography

**Albert Barnes,** *Barnes' Notes – The Gospels* (Baker Book House, Grand Rapids, MI; 1884 reprint)

**J. G. Bellett,** *The Evangelists, Meditations on the Four Gospels* (Bible Truth Publishers, Addison, IL; no date)

**F. W. Bruce,** *The Serious Christian, Notes on Hebrews* (Books for Christians, Charlotte, NC; no date)

**J. N. Darby,** The Holy Scriptures: A New Translation from the Original Languages (Logos Research Systems, Oak Harbor; 1996), electronic copy

**J. N. Darby,** *Synopsis of Books of the Bible Volumes 3 & 5* (Stow Hill Bible and Tract Depot, Kingston, ON; 1949)

**Edythe Draper,** *Draper's Quotations from the Christian World* (Tyndale House Publishers Inc., Wheaton, IL. – electronic copy)

**F. W. Grant,** *Genesis in the Light – The Serious Christian Series* (Loizeaux Brothers, Inc., Neptune, NJ)

**F. W. Grant,** *The Numerical Structure of Scripture* (Loizeaux Brothers, Bible Truth Depot, New York, NY; 7th printing 1956)

**David Gooding,** *According to Luke* (GOSPEL FOLIO PRESS, Port Colborne, ON; 1987)

**H. A. Ironside,** *Hebrews* (American Bible Conference; Philadelphia, PA; 1932)

**Andrew Jukes,** *Four Views of Christ* (Kregel Publications, Grand Rapids, MI; 1966)

**William Kelly,** *Introductory Lectures NT Vol. The Gospels* (Believers Book Shelf, Sunbury PA; 1970 reprint)

**William Kelly**, *The Serious Christian, Hebrews* (Books for Christians, Charlotte, NC; no date)

**L. Laurenson**, *Classic Christian Commentary* (Books for Christians, Charlotte, NC; no date)

**William MacDonald**, *Believer's Bible Commentary* (Thomas Nelsen Publishers, Nashville, TN; 1989)

**William MacDonald**, *Here's the Difference* (GOSPEL FOLIO PRESS, Port Colborne, ON; 1999)

**William G. Moorehead**, *The Fundamentals of Christianity: The Moral Glory of Jesus Christ* (Electronic Database. Copyright 1997 by Biblesoft)

**William Newell**, *Hebrews Verse by Verse* (Moody Press, Chicago, IL; 1947)

**Arthur Pink**, *Why Four Gospels?* (Scripture Truth Book Co., Fincastle, VA; no date)

**Samuel Ridout**, *The Serious Christian* (Books for Christians, Charlotte, NC; no date)

**A. T. Robertson**, *A Harmony of the Gospels* (Harper & Row Publishers, New York, NY; 1922)

**C. I. Scofield**, *The New Scofield Study Bible* (Oxford University Press, New York; 1967)

**Hamilton Smith**, *Classic Christian Commentary – Matthew* (Books for Christians, Charlotte, NC; no date)

**James Strong**, *New Exhaustive Strong's Numbers and Concordance with Expanded Greek-Hebrew Dictionary* (Biblesoft and International Bible Translators, Inc.; 1994), electronic copy

**Dr. Howard Taylor**, *Spiritual Secret of Hudson Taylor* (Whitaker House, New Kensington, PA; 1996)

**J. H. Thayer**, *Thayer's Greek Lexicon* (Biblesoft; 2000), electronic database

**John Walvoord**, *The Bible Knowledge Commentary* (Victor Books, Wheaton, IL; 1985)

**Warren Wiersbe**, *The Bible Exposition Commentary, Vol. 1* (Victor Books, Wheaton, IL; 1989)

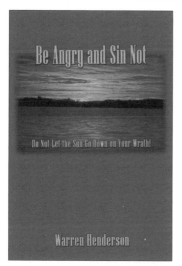

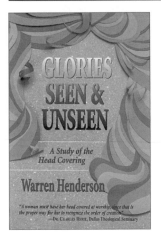

### GLORIES SEEN & UNSEEN

Should women cover her head while she is praying or during meetings of the church. What real significance does a head covering have in the 21st century anyway? Warren Henderson answers many questions about the Head Covering.

Binding: Paper
Category: Doctrine/Devotion
Page Count: 134
ISBN: 962838516X

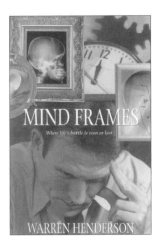

### MIND FRAMES

The author shares six scriptural exercises to strengthen the mind's ability to focus Godward and then presents a dozen Christlike attitudes—mind frames—to guard our thoughts in challenging circumstances.

Binding: Paper
Category: Discipleship
Page Count: 148
ISBN: 1882701941

# Warren Henderson

### SEEDS OF DESTINY

This is a devotional book which explores Genesis in relation to the rest of Scripture. It contains over 100 devotions, and is suitable as either a daily devotional or as a reference source for deeper study.

Binding: Hard Cover
Category: Devotional
Page Count: 390
ISBN: 1897117019

### YOUR HOME: A BIRTHING PLACE FOR HEAVEN?

A practical guide to evangelism at home and in the workplace.

Binding: Paper
Category: Practical/Ministry
Page Count: 144
ISBN: 1882701739

# BOOKS BY AUTHOR
# Neil M. Fraser

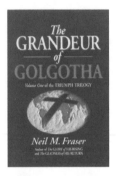

## THE GRANDEUR OF GOLGOTHA

Volume 1 of the Triumph Trilogy. If we sense that our devotion to Christ is not as it should be, we can rediscover our first love for Him where we first loved Him— at Calvary.

Binding: Paper          Page Count: 136
Category: Doctrine     ISBN: 1882701658

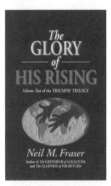

## THE GLORY OF HIS RISING

Volume 2 of the Triumph Trilogy gives Old Testament pictures of Christ's resurrection then follows this teaching through the New Testament writers.

Binding: Paper          Page Count: 144
Category: Doctrine     ISBN: 1882701674

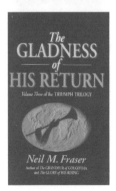

## THE GLADNESS OF HIS RETURN

Volume 3 of the Triumph Trilogy. Captivate your mind and heart with Old and New Testament texts pointing to His return. Purify your personal life, motivate evangelism, & feel joy as we await His coming again.

Binding: Paper          Page Count: 160
Category: Doctrine     ISBN: 1882701682

To Order Call: 1-800-952-2382 • orders@gospelfolio.com